The Objectivist M

MW00905718

The Ethical and Practical Case For Free Enterprise Capitalism

By: Stephen Long

Best wishes, Deborah!

STEVE

Foreword by Karis Saplys

DISCLAIMER: UNLESS OTHERWISE STATED, THE VIEWS EXPRESSED IN THE OBJECTIVIST MANIFESTO: THE ETHICAL AND PRACTICAL CASE FOR FREE ENTERPRISE CAPITALISM DO NOT NECESSARILY REFLECT THE VIEWS OF KEVIN POUNCE VILLARUZ, KARIS SAPLYS, AYN RAND, LEONARD PEIKOFF, HARRY BINSWANGER, NATHANIEL BRANDEN, CHARLES TEW, ERIC "SWORD OF APOLLO" M., YARON BROOK, PETER SCHIFF, LUDWIG VON MISES, LISA MORGAN-LONG, DAVID LONG, MALLORY LONG, NICHOLAS CATANIA, GEORGE MARION, OR ANY OTHER PERSON(S), COMPANIES OR ORGANIZATIONS AFFILIATED OR ASSOCIATED WITH IT.

Acknowledgements

The Objectivist Manifesto yields credit to the following individuals for spreading the ideas and philosophical discoveries making this book possible, even if its thesis does not agree with them all fully: Ayn Rand, Leonard Peikoff, Nathaniel Branden, Charles Tew, Harry Binswanger, Eric "Sword of Apollo" M., Yaron Brook, Peter Schiff, and Ludwig Von Mises.

The Objectivist Manifesto, however, is mostly an expansion upon the works of Ayn Rand and Leonard Peikoff. This book also yields extraordinary credit to both of my parents: Lisa Morgan-Long and David Long, for their gracious and continued support throughout the origination of this book, including their technical and editorial assistance. Without them, *The Objectivist Manifesto* would not have been possible. I would like to thank my friend Karis Saplys for his friendship over the span of nearly two decades, and almost my entire life. He was gracious enough to submit the foreword to this book, which brilliantly articulates the essence of capitalism, as well as the essence of its philosophical base. I would also like to thank Kevin Pounce Villaruz for providing the cover photograph of Abu Dhabi used in this very book. I would also like to thank my dear sister, Mallory Long, in addition to Nicholas Catania, George Marion, and many more!

Contents

Foreword

Throughout the course of history, men have fought and died for what they believe to be freedom or liberty. This has ensued since the time of Moses in Egypt, all the way to the birth of the United States of America. Wars have been fought and blood spilled in the name of this ideal.

But what does it mean to be free? It is a question which man has pondered since the dawn of civilization. By definition, freedom is a state of being in which an individual is not coerced, restrained, or otherwise hindered by some force of foreign domination, or tyrannical government. The questions that logically follow are: am I free? Are we free? Are any of us free in this day and age?

The idea put forth by the philosophy of Objectivism is that an individual's highest moral purpose is the pursuit of his or her own self-happiness. This moral theory, known as egoism, is the central pillar of the Objectivist philosophy, and understanding its fundamental implications are paramount to comprehending the hand-in-hand relationship Objectivism has with free market capitalism.

Throughout *The Objectivist Manifesto*, Stephen Long expertly applies Objectivism to concrete aspects of society, providing practical, real-world solutions to the constant encroachment of collectivism and economic enslavement that grows seemingly by the day in the West. *The Objectivist Manifesto: The Ethical and Practical Case For Free Enterprise Capitalism* serves as a clarion call to those tired of stagnant political discourse, and who seek to put an end to the infringements on the rights of man that have become common actions of modern-day governments.

Being myself a long-time friend of Stephen Long, I have always known him to be a man of principle. He is steadfast and unwavering in his exaltation of reason, and unmatched in his dedication to individualism and freedom. I can safely say there is no individual better equipped to pass the torch of Objectivism and individual liberty on to the next generation of impactful men and women. If there is one person that can convince someone of the virtue of selfishness, it is he. To conclude, in the words of Ayn Rand; "*If you know that this life is all that you have, wouldn't you make the most of it?*" Stephen Long and *The Objectivist Manifesto* invite the reader to do just that.

Introduction

This is the theory:

"We are socialists, we are enemies of today's capitalistic economic system for the **exploitation of the economically weak, with its unfair salaries, with its unseemly evaluation of a human being according to wealth and property** instead of responsibility and performance, and we are all determined to destroy this system under all conditions" - Adolf Hitler, 1927 [bolding added] (Williamson 180).

"...In the working out of a great national program which seeks the primary good of the greater number, it is true that the toes of some people are being stepped on and are going to be stepped on. But these toes belong to **the comparative few who seek to retain or to gain position or riches or both by some shortcut which is harmful to the greater good**." - Franklin D. Roosevelt, June 1934 [bolding added] (Wikiquote).

" ...**if you've been successful, you didn't get there on your own**... I'm always struck by people who think, well, it must be because I was just so smart... If you were successful, somebody along the line gave you some help... Somebody helped to create this unbelievable American system that we have that allowed you to thrive. Somebody invested in roads and bridges. **If you've got a business — you didn't build that**. Somebody else made

that happen. The Internet didn't get invented on its own. Government research created the Internet so that all the companies could make money off the Internet… We rise or fall together as one nation and as one people, and that's the reason I'm running for President — because I still believe in that idea. You're not on your own, we're in this together". - Barack Obama, July 13, 2012 [bolding added] (*Fact Check*).

The modern era, including the 20th and 21st centuries, has been riddled with a countless number of mindless and irrational attacks against free enterprise. The system is blamed for succumbing to an array of ethical and practical faults, including those faults which are mutually exclusive. Peace activists blame free enterprise for causing profit-driven "corporate warfare". Simultaneously, fascists blame it for succumbing to "bourgeois pacifism", and being insufficient for "moral adventure". Feminist and queer activists, who accuse it of reinforcing "patriarchal" gender and social norms, blame free enterprise for being oppressive and sexist. Simultaneously, the Neo-reactionaries blame it for encouraging "sexual degeneracy", and being "dysgenic" to society. Free enterprise is accused of spreading and enabling racism. "Alt-Right" activists blame it for the degradation of "racial identity", and enabling multiculturalism. Fascists blame free enterprise for causing people to lose their connection to their community, becoming parasitic and antisocial. Yet Marxists blame it for causing people to lose connection to their individuality, through the process of "alienation".

If A is A, then A cannot also be non-A at the same time and in the same respect. Either free enterprise is too violent, or too peaceful. It is either too prudish, or too libertine. It is either too racist, or too individualistic. It is either too "atomizing", or too domineering. The opponents of free enterprise blame it for succumbing to each side of each dichotomy that they present, without any regard for its actual nature. Free enterprise is under attack from every angle, and is blamed for everything it can be mindlessly accused of causing. An alleged humanitarianism, compassion, pacifism, or justice does not motivate the opponents of free enterprise. The opponents of free enterprise are at philosophical war against freedom, and its necessary source: egoism.

The thesis put forth by *The Objectivist Manifesto* is that free enterprise is the only social system compatible with the rights of man, and thus is the only type of society fit to the life of a rational being. Free enterprise is the social system that represents the recognition of all rights, including property rights, in their full, consistent, absolute application. At its core, free enterprise protects the cause and effect relationship between one's mind and external reality, by securing the individual's exclusive right to the product of his/her mind, which is embodied in both intellectual and physical property rights. It is also the only social system, which embodies the legal implementation of individual rights; placing a ban on the initiation of physical force in human relationships from all agents, including government agents. The government in this system may only retaliate against rights violations, or threats thereof, and has no power to infringe upon individual rights in any capacity. Free enterprise is also the only just system; every agent is rewarded or punished based on the rationality of his/her actions, and must bear the full consequences thereof. There is no systematic moral hazard; no agent can escape the effects of his/her own irrationality. Due to these reasons, in addition to many others, free enterprise is the social system best equipped to allowing agents to pursue egoistic values, become successful, and achieve happiness.

Free enterprise is the only social system compatible with individual rights, and is thus the only ethical and practical social system for human existence. None of the other three political ideologies: anarchism, communism, or fascism, or anything in between can ever parallel, let alone surpass its freedom, prosperity, and benevolence. Free enterprise is *not* "pragmatic", or "the best of the worst", as argued by conservatives. That is not to say that it is impractical; Ayn Rand herself noted that the moral *is* the practical. Instead, it is radically egoistic, individualistic, and rights-based. It is not a disintegrated amalgamation of *ad hoc* policy points. It is systematic and rigorous; it is a ruthlessly logical and integrated political philosophy aimed at devising the proper social system for rational beings. It is not a collection of political slogans and bumper stickers; it is a sober and realistic view of both government and the economy, taking into consideration many insights from Austrian and supply-side economics. It is well informed about the nature of rights by its egoist ethical base, and is ruthlessly diligent in applying those rights fully, consistently, and absolutely. It is from this base that it derives its radical political conclusions. Any other method of deriving them is worse than mere falsehood; it is truth by accident.

There still remain some defenders of free enterprise, even after the centuries of philosophical assault against it, but most are so ill-equipped to defending it philosophically that they are actually *destructive* to the very cause that they purport to be supporting. Conservatives attempt to defend free enterprise by tying it to religious mysticism and mindless obedience. By doing so, conservatives surrender this world to statism, and instead attempt to flee into a supernatural dimension. Libertarians attempt to uphold free enterprise by tying it to whim-worshipping subjectivism and the chaos of anarchy. The result is the opposite of liberty; anarchy represents the proliferation, not elimination, of violence and tyranny. Neo-reactionaries tie free enterprise to the crude collectivism of racism and self-sacrificial duty. Such a base is akin to fascism, not a system of individual rights. In order to save free enterprise, one must promote it on the grounds of reason, egoism, and as a consequence, individualism. One must recognize that the only justification for free enterprise is the premise that rational beings have the moral right and purpose to pursue their own selfish interests. It is only from this base that one can conclude that such beings should be free from coercion and force. To cooperate with any of the three aforementioned groups: conservatives, libertarians, reactionaries, is to abandon the philosophical base of free enterprise, and is thus to betray one's own future.

In contrast to these three groups, Objectivism does not regard politics as being a separate matter to more fundamental philosophical contexts. It regards free enterprise as being the logical political implementation of its ethics: egoism. Objectivists are not "conservatives", but radical capitalists. Upholding a completely laissez-faire, unregulated free market in which the only role of the government is to protect individual rights, Objectivists necessarily advocate a complete separation of state and economy. Objectivists prescribe the privatization of all aspects of the economy, encompassing production, distribution, and trade.

One could read *The Objectivist Manifesto* as a continuation of Ayn Rand's *Capitalism: The Unknown Ideal*, or as an Objectivist version of Christopher Rachels's *A Spontaneous Order: The Capitalist Case For a Stateless Society*; although rejecting Christopher Rachels' anarchism, *The Objectivist Manifesto* takes some of his insight in the practical utility of private property. *The Objectivist Manifesto* is built upon the epistemological and ethical premises outlined in Ayn Rand's *Introduction to Objectivist Epistemology* and *The Virtue of Selfishness*, respectively.

The Objectivist Manifesto is not a complete summary or explanation of Objectivism, its premises, or its conclusions. Rather than reinventing the wheel, *The Objectivist Manifesto* is tasked with applying Objectivism's politics to concrete aspects of society. Those curious about the philosophical origin of this book ought to read *Objectivism: The Philosophy of Ayn Rand* by Leonard Peikoff.

The Objectivist Manifesto is aimed at explaining, in ruthlessly precise detail, the practical, political implications of Ayn Rand's unique philosophy: Objectivism. While not a dusty tome of paper and ink, *The Objectivist Manifesto* remains very comprehensive in just over one hundred pages, discussing a wide range of topics, including government, banking, healthcare, the environment, and many more! Liberals beware - *The Objectivist*

Manifesto is liable to radically alter your understanding of morality, government, and the free market.

As you read through every page of this book, I encourage you to be sceptical of every proposition that I make; never take my word on faith or without sufficient proof. I also encourage you to apply this same level of scepticism to contemporary political trends, and allow your reason and objectivity to supersede your comfort in familiarity.

The true cause of the backlash against free enterprise in America is a culture of intellectual and moral bankruptcy, unaware of and uninterested in the system's moral base. The cultural dominance of this attitude has resulted in the slow and gradual mutilation, disfiguration, and ruination of individual liberty. *The Objectivist Manifesto* is aimed at anyone sickened by this trend towards collectivism and enslavement, and who yearn for a world of individualism and freedom. It is aimed at those with free minds and strong spirits: those who know that there is an alternative to tyranny, and who aren't ready to give up.

Selfishness is virtuous. Freedom is possible. Independence is real.

Part One: Theory

Chapter 1: Ethics

Due to the radical nature of Objectivism, in addition to its unconventional premises and goals, its political implications cannot be discussed without first explaining its radically unconventional approach to ethics. Objectivism does not start on the philosophical base of 21st century America, and simply extrapolate the culture's implicit political conclusions based on those premises. If it did, it would be completely apprehended from ever reaching the truth. It would be forever lost in whatever direction the culture happens to go, without any reference to fundamental principles about the nature of ethics, and the implications of those principles in politics. In that case, Objectivism would be the most pathetic, trite, ineffective political philosophy, manipulated by distortions and false premises, and walked off a cliff blindfolded into complete tyranny. In other words, it would become liberalism.

In analysing the philosophical branch of ethics, it is important to start from the beginning, without any assumptions and taking nothing for granted about the nature of the field. Every conclusion in ethics, akin to every other field of study, must be *proved*. Morality is not an excuse to evade reality or inject mysticism. In fact, doing either of those things will inevitably lead one to the *wrong* conclusions. Rather, Objectivism builds its ethical framework

from the bottom up, taking the most basic facts about existence, and logically

extrapolating their inescapable ethical conclusions, holding reason to be its

only absolute. (The validity of reason can be demonstrated axiomatically, and

it is not necessary, in this discussion to refer to metaphysical or

epistemological analysis).

The Problem of Ethics

Philosophically, ethics is perceived either to be a consequence of

mysticism, or is otherwise disregarded as having no connection or

relationship to reality. Most atheist philosophers, whether explicitly or

implicitly, directly or tacitly, have endorsed the idea that ethics is nothing

more than the product of human consciousness, and have regarded it as either

a mystic fantasy or arbitrary postulate, disconnected from any and all

objective facts. Based on their shared premise that ethics has no objective

relationship to reality, these individuals conclude that there is no absolute

right or wrong in any context.

While regarded as the opposite of this view, religious mysticism held

a similar stance. According to religious mystics, it is the omniscient dictates

of *God*(s) that determines the ultimate standard of ethics, rather than any reference to reality. They treat moral teachings as mystically revealed, out-of-context absolutes with no relationship to rational beings. But since the concept "God" refers to a being instead of reality, the ethics of religious mysticism actually refer to God's subjectivism. Akin to nihilists, religious mystics also evade the objective nature of values, and its relationship to rational beings. Thus, religious mysticism merely pushes the problem of ethics back a step; it is completely unequipped to answer the fundamental question: "is ethics necessary? If so, why?"

The Solution to The Problem of Ethics

The solution to the problem of ethics is deceptively simple. In contrast to both nihilistic subjectivism and religious mysticism, Ayn Rand's ethics proved and articulated an *objective* basis for ethics; morality based on and derived from the objective relationship between human consciousness and external reality. What Ayn Rand's ethics recognized is that ethics is inescapable; it is an *objective, metaphysical necessity* of human survival of which without, human life is impossible. Ayn Rand recognized that human survival is not automatic, and thus requires a specific code of values. It was only after Rand proved the necessity of a code of ethics that she was able to deduce the *proper* code of ethics for humans; one which holds the self's life as its ultimate standard of value, and happiness as its ultimate goal. Since the purpose of ethics is to uphold human life, the proper code of ethics is one that maximizes the quality of an individual's life. Since it is proper to a being's existence to promote one's own life, beings should act in a way conducive to achieving that goal. Philosophically, it is impossible to get any deeper than that.

This also philosophically demonstrates the evil of altruism: it demands that a moral agent act against one's own life. Since acting against one's own life is improper to a rational agent's existence, altruism cannot be justified as a code of values to guide a being's existence. This same principle holds true for religious ethics, utilitarianism, deontology, stoicism, pragmatic ethics, and hedonism, which all demand, in at least some circumstances, that one acts against one's own life. However, these ideologies are not as committed to this principle - and therefore are not as evil - as altruism.

The Objectivist Ethics

The logical conclusion of all of Rand's premises is rational egoism. Egoism holds that moral agents ought to do what is in their rational self-interest, in order to maximize their happiness throughout the entire course of their lives. Egoism is a consequentialist, agent-positive position of ethics, which requires the prioritization of one's own life and interests over the interests of others. This does *not* mean that one should attempt to gain at the expense of others: fraud, theft, etc. for two reasons.

The first reason is that Ayn Rand's ethics are based on the premise that humans are rational beings, and therefore they cannot survive as some animals do: by following their impulses. Since the use of physical force neutralizes reason: humans' basic means of survival and only means of gaining knowledge, such behaviour is unfit to the life of a rational being.

Additionally, the use of force is a monstrous contradiction according to egoism: since one's right and purpose to pursue one's interests is derived from one's nature as a rational being, any particular rational agent must apply this principle universally to all other rational beings; i.e. to recognize all rational beings' rights to pursue their interests without the interference of physical force. If a rational being does not do this, but believes that he still has rights, he is being logically inconsistent and creating an ethical *double standard*. If, instead, a rational being denies the rights of himself and others, and plunders and destroys like a barbarian, he sabotages his own rational faculty, reducing himself to the position of an animal, and thus contradicts the very principle of egoism: reason. By initiating force against others, a rational being implicitly endorses the initiation of force against oneself. But since force is improper to the existence of a rational being, one endorses what one knows to be destructive to one's own life.

The rights derived from rational egoism do not apply to non-rational animals, nor do they apply to robots, plants, fungi, or amoeba. They only apply to beings which utilize independent rational thought as its primary means of survival; i.e., a being to which the initiation of physical force is improper.

The moral implication of egoism is that moral agents ought to do what is objectively to one's own benefit throughout the entire course of one's existence. Thus, one must never sacrifice one's own life to the whims or demands of others. One should be laser-focused on pursuing one's own interests, and maximizing one's own long-term quality of life. One must act in a manner maximally conducive to the goal of ethics: happiness, which Ayn Rand defined as a state of "non-contradictory joy", i.e. a state of pleasure perfectly aligned with one's quality of life.

Egoism's fundamental virtue is rationality, from which its other five virtues are derived. Based on it, one must always recognize that the unreal is unreal and therefore cannot be of any value to any being: the virtue of honesty (1). One must always recognize what one has accomplished and what one hasn't, and must never attempt to gain a value fraudulently or illegitimately: the virtue of justice (2). One must always act in accordance with one's own convictions: the virtue of integrity (3). One must attempt to gain self-serving value through the independent use of one's mind: the virtue of productiveness (4). Finally, one must always take satisfaction in one's own accomplishments, and must always recognize the efficacy of one's own mind: the virtue of pride (5).

The Nature of Values

Since Ayn Rand's ethics are egoistic, rejecting both subjectivism and intrinsicism, it also has a completely unconventional approach to values. Ayn Rand recognized that values are neither a product of rational consciousness disintegrated from reality (subjectivism), nor are values an attribute of reality disintegrated from rational consciousness (intrinsicism). Instead, values are *Objective*. In order to be a value, a decision or existent must be objectively beneficial to a being's life; mindlessly self-destructive whims achieve the opposite of what values do. Instead of enabling a being to achieve one's own rational self-interest, it makes the achievement of one's self-interest *more* difficult. Instead of promoting a being's life, self-destructive whim sabotages it. A value must also be based on a being's rational, volitional action; if a decision or existent is forced upon a rational being, then that being becomes entirely disconnected from the "value" in question. A forceful imposition of an existent or decision, regardless of whether it is objectively beneficial to a being's life, subverts and undercuts the means by which beings achieve values: reason. Thus, the existent or decision cannot be a value; the being did not act to achieve it. In essence, self-destructive whim sabotages the end consequence of values: promoting a being's life. Forceful imposition of values or existents, in contrast, subverts and undercuts the means by which beings achieve values: reason. In order to be a value to a being, an existent or decision must be objectively beneficial to a being's life, but it also must be based on that being's volitional action. Put in simpler terms, it must be correct *and* chosen. Thus, Objectivism rejects both libertinism and authoritarianism, recognizing them both to be immoral and corrupt. Based upon this theory of values, Objectivism meets its inescapable political conclusions, which regards freedom *and* morality as being both inseparable corollaries and prerequisites for achieving any and all ethical values. Objectivism upholds a political system, which both allows agents within it to be free from coercion, and is most conducive for agents to achieve ethical values.

Chapter 2: Property

The political implementation of Objectivism can be summarized in two words: free enterprise. Since the moral good for a rational being is to pursue one's own interests through independent, rational effort, it is also critical that such beings are able to keep the tangible results of that effort. The proper legal implementation of the effect or product of that effort is twofold: intellectual property and physical property rights. The purpose of both intellectual property and physical property rights is to protect the cause and effect relationship between intellectual or physical effort, and the product of that effort. In a metaphysical sense, it is the legal protection of the relationship between reason and survival.

Property rights, whether intellectual or physical, ensure that moral agents always remain the beneficiary of their own rationally self-interested, productive actions. If someone forcefully seizes the possession or use of an unearned value from the originator (the process of theft), then that person, in effect, forces the originator of that value, unknowingly, to altruistically self-sacrifice for the sake of the illegitimate beneficiary. As the cause and effect relationship between effort and product is breached, the originator of the value is enslaved to the beneficiary. This demonstrates why property rights are the corollary to political freedom. It also demonstrates the inseparable connection between ethics and politics: property rights are a corollary to egoism, but are incompatible with altruism.

Rights are integrated in a logical, linear fashion. The most fundamental right is the right to life, being proper to a being's existence. But in order to live, a being must be able to take the actions, which sustain one's own life: the right to liberty. In order for self-serving actions to be meaningful, a being must be able to keep the exclusive use of its product: the right to property. If a being cannot dispose of its property, it cannot dispose of its effort. If it cannot dispose of its effort, it cannot dispose of its life.

Intellectual Property

Intellectual property is the primary implementation of property, while physical property is the derivative implementation. All property is fundamentally intellectual, since its creation requires the exercise of independent, rational effort. Physical property rights are merely intellectual property rights applied to concretized physical values.

Intellectual property is a unique form of property in that it cannot legitimately be inherited by one's successors. This is due to what intellectual property and physical property abstractly represent. Intellectual property is the legal implementation of the right to the direct product of one's mind: the origination of an idea. Physical property is the legal implementation of an idea's derivative: concretized physical values. Since to inherit something is to gain it directly from another, and since intellectual property represents the right to an idea, to inherit intellectual property would imply that one can simply inherit the content of a predecessor's mind. This, however, is a factual error; one cannot inherit the content of someone else's mind (intellectual property), either by default or decree. However, one can inherit its derivative, concretized result (physical property).

Additionally, intellectual property cannot be legitimately traded or sold to any person(s) for essentially the same reason. To allow this, the law would declare, in effect, that someone can trade away the content of his/her mind, even though it is not physiologically possible, since one has a direct connection to their own mind. If technology advances to a point in which the direct exchange of mental content is possible, then such transfer or inheritance of intellectual property would make perfect sense. However, as of the present day, this is not possible, and so the law should reflect this current reality. It is important to remember that laws are *contextual* absolutes. They do not always apply, but when they do apply, they apply absolutely.

This does not mean, however, that the originator of intellectual property cannot invite others to use it in exchange for material compensation. Within free enterprise, licensing agreements between various companies regarding the use of intellectual property would abound, so long as they are mutually beneficial to all parties involved. There is nothing illegitimate in such a practice, since the intellectual property in this scenario is not separated from the originator. The only rule is: the exclusive use of intellectual property cannot be transferred *from* the originator, as is currently embodied in exclusive distribution rights. Within free enterprise, all intellectual property is contingent upon the originator, and is thus necessarily dependant on the originator. Furthermore, intellectual property cannot ever be *separated* from the originator.

Because intellectual property is contingent on its originator or creator, all patents, copyrights, etc. should last for the entire duration of the creator's lifetime, unless the creator wants to pre-emptively terminate the patent, copyright, etc. (The creator, however, would need to pay commensurate fees in order to retain his/her exclusive production rights). No creator is obligated to patent or copyright his/her work; if the creator wants others to be able to use, remix, etc. the product of his/her mind, then he/she can leave it within the public domain. If he/she does choose to patent or copyright his/her work, however, his/her patent or copyright must be based on the evidence of his/her contribution, not merely his/her verbal claim. Additionally, there can also be multiple owners of a patent or copyright, so long as they all contributed to the origination of that enterprise. For example, if a mutualistic enterprise works together on the origination of a syphilis-curing drug, then they should be credited as a group with exclusive intellectual ownership of it. In this case, the drug patent would last for each contributor the duration of his/her lifetime.

Intellectual property can only apply to *inventions*, not *discoveries*. This is due to the fact, as mentioned before, that the purpose of intellectual property is the legal implementation of one's right to the product of one's mind. A discovery is not the product of one's mind; since reality is objective, it exists whether or not humans or any rational being is aware of it. Thus, no rational being can honestly claim to have *created* it. For example, one cannot attempt to copyright the physical law of entropy. One can copyright the book, article, video, recording, etc. in which they outline and explain the law of entropy, but not the scientific fact itself. An invention on the other hand, is completely contingent upon a rational agent to have brought it into existence. Thus, the protection of such a cause-effect relationship is completely legitimate. For example, if one creates a device designed to measure the physical law of entropy, a patent for it is legitimate.

Physical Property

Physical property is the derivative of intellectual property, applied to concretized physical values. Instead of being created through a process of *invention*, as is the case with intellectual property, physical property is created through a process of physical appropriation. Its contextual basis, rather than being created out of thin air, is derived from the effort of a moral agent *applied* to a scarce physical good. In this manner, a moral agent mixes one's labour with the good in order to put it to productive use for its life. Physical property can only be acquired legitimately in four ways: (1) original appropriation (including after previous abandonment), (2) voluntary exchange, (3) inheritance, and (4) criminal compensation. Otherwise, such an acquisition of property necessarily violates the property rights of others, and such ill-gotten gains would therefore be illegitimate.

The owner of physical property has the right to the exclusive use of that good for as long as it remains in his/her possession. The owner of physical property can temporarily renounce exclusive use of it if he/she wishes to invite others to use it, temporarily. The owner of physical property can also permanently renounce exclusive or total ownership of it, by providing shares of the property, or by giving it away, respectively. However, the owner of property cannot be *forced* to invite others onto it, or to yield exclusive or total ownership.

The owner of physical property may bar access or use of that good to any number of individuals of his/her choosing. The owner of physical property can establish fences, walls, security, etc. to physically repel and remove trespassers. However, these methods of repulsion must be proportionate to the offence of trespassing. Even if someone really *does* trespass on private property, shooting them with a tomahawk missile is still murder. Non-owners of private property can interact with it in any way that does not limit the owner's exclusive use of it. For example, one *can* project radio waves through someone else's property, since this does not limit the owner's exclusive use of it. However, one *cannot* blast deafening sound or blinding light onto someone else's property, since it would limit the owner's exclusive use of it.

The owner of physical property *cannot* legitimately imprison another agent on its premises. This is due to the fact that imprisonment, unlike removal or repulsion, prevents an agent from being able to not interact with that good. The owner of physical property can prevent others from interacting with it, but cannot force others to interact with it. The first is the protection of one's own goods, while the second is enslavement. The only exception to this rule is if such apprehension or imprisonment is used as a form of self-defence against an attacker, if government agents are currently unavailable. This is justified because the context of the imprisonment has fundamentally changed; Instead of using imprisonment to destroy human life, one is using it to neutralize destruction, and consequently to protect one's own life.

Property Abandonment

Physical property, in addition to intellectual property, must also be subjected to time limits. Physical property is the legal implementation of the right to the product of one's effort. As long as that effort is commensurate with the physical property, ownership for it is legitimate. However, if that effort is erased via negligence or abandonment, one cannot retain legitimate ownership of that property. In a free, competitive society, no one would long retain ownership of an abandoned estate or good. Some types of property have automatic time limits; organic matter will disintegrate, and certain land estates can be reclaimed by nature. Since all property is contingent on the effort of the originator, its ownership cannot be unconditionally eternal.

Physical property could theoretically be eternal, as long as the originator and successors exercise commensurate effort. However, without such commensurate effort the legal implementation of that property becomes meaningless.

The Utility of Property

In addition to embodying the legal implementation of an agent's right to the product of one's mind, private property is also an extremely useful tool for incentivizing - and even enforcing - rational, productive behaviour without violating individual rights. This concept is currently embodied in the idea of "covenant communities", in which a group of property owners dissuade individuals from engaging in self-destructive behaviour, either through barring such behaviour from their properties, or through voluntary dissociation. This practice is both legitimate and beneficial, so long as it does not impose such restrictions upon the person(s) or property of others.

Absent government infringements upon private property, society tends to spontaneously self-regulate according to objective economic value. The ethics of rational self-interest, which is embodied in the free enterprise system, motivates individuals to make rational, productive choices instead of short-sighted, self-destructive ones. Free enterprise is based on the principle that no agent may seize an unearned value from another. The consequence of this basic principle is a void of moral hazard; each individual must bear the full consequences of one's own decisions, and cannot simply defer responsibility onto an innocent victim. Individuals may rely on voluntary charity, but this is only possible to the extent that they are admired or sympathetic to others. Voluntary charity will aid the sympathetic and genuinely disadvantaged, but it will not aid the irrational and dastardly.

Private property - a concept in its full legal implementation exclusive to free enterprise - is the only thing that makes complete political freedom possible. Freedom entails the possibility of making the wrong choices. In order to learn what the right and wrong choices are, individuals must be faced with the consequences of those choices. The free market, therefore, acts as the teacher or mentor of rational beings. If beings act in a manner conducive to their long-term self-interest, they will be endowed with reward, as a consequence of the nature of reality. If beings act in a manner contrary to their long-term self-interest, they will face negative consequences, and will be able to see the effects of their mistakes with full clarity. Thus, free enterprise is the social system with the greatest incentive to be rationally self-interested, and is thus most conducive to achieving ethical values.

Contract

Another important aspect of free enterprise, besides physical and intellectual property is contract. A contract, for reference, is a legal agreement outlining a specific trade or exchange of values between multiple agents, including labour, capital, etc. Contract is the means by which rational agents are able to achieve both economic predictability, and trade on a scale otherwise impossible. For this reason, many regard contract as the basis for civilization itself. A contract only has validity if it was agreed to voluntarily; no one can legitimately be *forced* to sign a contract of any kind, or have a contract imposed upon them. However, once signed, law can legitimately enforce a contract; the breach of such a document would constitute the violation of one's will, and is fraudulent in nature. Thus, at such a point it is legitimate to pursue compensation for such a breach, and would be a matter for civil court. However, one cannot write in any mindless, arbitrary punishment into a contract; if a business, for example, writes crucifixion into a contract as punishment for a breach, a government cannot legitimately enforce this. A government *can* enforce financial compensation for such a breach, but it *cannot* enforce irrational, disproportionate punishments for breach of contract.

Chapter 3: Government

Free enterprise is the only system compatible with individual rights. It is, in effect, the only social system that bans the initiation of physical force in human relationships. This means that human relationships within free enterprise are completely based on voluntary consent, rather than coercion and violence. Free enterprise is the only social system, which allows one to keep the product of one's own effort, and thus the product of one's mind. Thus, in the free enterprise system, all forms of production, distribution, and trade are subject to private ownership. Free enterprise is a system in which the sole purpose of the government is to protect individual rights, and one in which the government is legally banned from taking any action which violates the rights of others, or making any compromises on individual rights. In effect, there are only three functions that a proper government within free enterprise fulfils: defence, legal arbitration, and criminal punishment. In modern, practical application, these mean the equivalent of: police, military, law courts, and prisons. Its role would be that of a policeman, protecting individual rights according to objective legal principles.

The Objectivist Government

The form of government that is the most effective at achieving the above, curbing corruption and resisting creeping tyranny is a constitutional republic. A constitutional republic is a system of government based on a specific code of laws, rather than the whims of specific agents, and thus recognizes the primacy of individual rights to the greatest extent out of all possible types. In other words, a constitutional republic represents the rule of law, rather than the rule of people. This is because it prevents both the majority and elected officials from creating policies, which would infringe upon rights in any capacity.

Political officials within a constitutional republic are indeed elected through a majority vote. Thus, a constitutional republic is often said to be democratic. However, it is fundamentally different from all other forms of democracy in that it puts the right to vote within its sole proper political context: keeping political officials accountable. If a president within a constitutional republic is caught attempting to use power for corrupt and unjust purposes, he/she can simply be rotated out through the electoral process. However, as alluded to earlier, the right to vote does not apply to everything. For example, within a constitutional republic, the 51% majority of the population cannot simply vote to kill the 49% minority; this would be mass murder. Instead, a fundamental set of legal principles based on individual rights would be required in a government's legal system in order for it to resist every inch of tyranny.

Law and Justice

Because a free enterprise society is based on strict adherence to individual rights, every single law enforced by the government would exist for the explicit, sole purpose of protecting them. This principle applies to its most fundamental protections outlined in its constitution, as outlined earlier, all the way down to its narrowest rules and ordinances. More specifically, the law would prohibit murder, assault, rape, theft, destruction or vandalism of property, breach of contract, breach of intellectual property, privacy invasion, fraud, threats of violence, criminal abetting, slander, libel, criminal deception, and (certain types of) criminal negligence.

The fundamental principle upon which these laws are based is more important than any particular law. Essentially, any act, which constitutes the initiation of physical force, would be illegal in a free enterprise society. Any act, which does not constitute the initiation of physical force, cannot be and is not a crime. Thus, acts such as drug use, prostitution, holocaust denial, public nudity, etc. would all be legalized and unregulated. This does not necessarily tell individuals if they *should* participate in these acts; it is the task of ethics to answer such questions. But what it *does* mean is that individuals will not be put under the threat of violent oppression for participating in such actions.

Every law within a free enterprise society must also be objective, predictable, and impeccably precise. One should be able to have *absolute* certainty before taking an action whether or not it will be illegal, *why* it is illegal, and what the consequences of taking that action will be. This is also a commensurate aspect to individual rights; if a law is whimsical or unpredictable, it is also tyrannical and oppressive.

Criminal Punishment

Within free enterprise, criminal punishment would be much more focused on restitution (and occasionally incapacitation) than it would be on retribution, rehabilitation, deterrence, etc. In a free, rational society, victims of crime would be much more likely to seek material compensation rather than the fleeting, expedient emotional relief of retribution. Retribution is a primitive form of justice that has a tendency to be counterproductive and hazardous. It consists of inflicting harm upon a perpetrator in order to achieve symmetry with the victim. While giving serial rapists a "taste of their own medicine" might give one a positive feeling of righteous vindication, it would also achieve nothing positive, give no benefit to the victim besides fleeting emotional gain, and could very well lead to more psychological damage to the rapist, giving him/her the very feelings of inadequacy and insecurity that often *leads* to rape in the first place. Thus, retribution actually makes re-assimilation for criminals *more* difficult.

Retribution is also hazardous in that it runs the risk of becoming disproportionate to the crime committed, especially if those within a justice system are emotionally biased against the offender. Finally, retribution, especially capital punishment is hazardous in that it risks inflicting physical and psychological harm upon the innocently convicted, making them *more* likely to commit crime. This is especially true of capital punishment, which risks opening the door to state *murder*. This is not just a hazard in theory: According to the National Academy of Sciences of the United States of America, at *least* 4.1%, or approximately 1 in every 25 death penalty defendants executed are innocently convicted in the United States (National Academy of Sciences). One innocent defendant executed should *alone* be outrageous. The fact that capital punishment commits murder 4.1% of the time is so appalling that it is difficult to describe.

This should not be taken as support for criminal rehabilitation either. Violations of individual rights should not be met with disproportionate annihilation, but they should also not be met with compassion or sympathy. A crime, unless accidental, is an act of explicit evil that must be dealt with seriously and prudently. Giving a mass murderer a stay in a 5-star hotel is *not* a rational response to such an act. To treat it as one is so crass an evasion that even to give it the benefit of the doubt is beyond obscene, and is indistinguishable from the appeasement of criminals. Rehabilitation is an ineffective and irrational strategy for dealing with crime.

Restitution, unlike retribution and rehabilitation, is an effective, rational, productive, and secure manner of dealing with crime. Restitution is the process of forcing a criminal offender to compensate the victim(s) of his/her crime(s), in an attempt to restore whatever the victim(s) lost to the perpetrator. This compensation can be provided in the form of monetary compensation, physical or mental labour, or other valuable goods equivalent to the damage of the crime. Restitution, adhering to the basic principle of a free enterprise society, the non-initiation of force, must be symmetrical to the crime committed. If it becomes disproportionate to the crime committed, then the punishment itself becomes an offence. Forcing petty vandals to labour for their entire lives isn't proper criminal justice, but slavery.

Unlike the other forms of criminal punishment, restitution allows the victim to gain back approximately what they lost to the offender, such that any given person has to worry very little about becoming a victim of crime. In a retributive or rehabilitative system, a victim is much more vulnerable to the pernicious effects of crime, because they will not be recompensed for their suffering. They know that they will be safe from another offence from that specific criminal, albeit temporarily, but they will still be damaged from it, and thus any offence against them will be much more likely to ruin them.

Finally, if a criminal is innocently convicted via restitution, then the compensation process can simply be reversed, rather than them being physically or psychologically damaged, or killed. This makes restitution much more secure as a manner of dealing with crime.

Some may object to restitution on the grounds that it is incapable of addressing some of the most serious crimes, such as rape, murder, etc., and that no restitution can ever undo such a crime, or bring back a loved one. Observe how the critics of restitution hold it to such an unreasonable standard of effectiveness. It is true that the government does not have the metaphysical might to simply undo crimes, nor is any material restitution preferable to the absence of the offence. However, restitution is the only form of criminal punishment that is able to give the victims of crime some means of satisfying their desires, rather than the fleeting emotional satisfaction of vindication. Restitution can make reparations for crimes committed in some capacity. It is not perfect, but it is superior to retribution or rehabilitation.

If a criminal continuously reoffends or offends severely to the extent that he/she has to be regarded as a threat to the rest of society, then incapacitation may become necessary. Incapacitation is a theory of criminal justice, which prescribes the physical removal of dangerous individuals from the rest of society, so long as they are a physical threat to others. Incapacitation may also be necessary for individuals with contagious disease(s) radiating from their person(s) such that they become a physical threat to others. These individuals would be held in quarantine, however, instead of prisons. The use of incapacitation should be rare; the overwhelming majority of people are not eminent threats to others, and would tend to be deterred from crime via restitutive punishment. However, for those whom to which it is necessary, it should be instituted for as long as necessary; until it can be proved that the criminal in question is no longer a physical threat to others. When exactly incapacitation should be instituted is a complex issue, and requires a precise evaluation of the specific criminal's probability to reoffend, and the extent to which that criminal's re-offense would damage the lives of others. As with many legal issues, it is difficult to determine the answer with complete precision in every case, and would likely be best decided by a precedent-based, common law system. What is most important in regards to the issue of incapacitation is whether or not the government is *essentially* acting to protect individual rights.

Government Financing

A proper government would also be prohibited from using the two appalling forms of financing used by governments historically and presently: taxation and inflation. Taxation is the more obviously evil form of government financing, which consists of the criminal process of coerced extraction or theft of money from non-violent, non-guilty, non-criminals. Taxation violates property rights - the fundamental principle of free enterprise - and therefore cannot be justified. The incompatibility between taxation and property rights inescapably entails that taxation would have no place in a society based on individual rights.

Inflation is a less noticeable, albeit equally evil form of government financing. It consists of the process of legalized counterfeiting, in which a government prints or manufactures excess money in order to finance its own services. This process reduces the value of the specific currency in question for all owners of such a currency, robbing the owners of their legitimately earned economic value. This duplicitous process cannot be justified or tolerated; its invisibility does not make it any better than taxation.

In order to be a just, dignified defender of individual rights, a government must collect all its financing *voluntarily*. The only rule is: the government may not initiate the use of physical force against any person(s). Initiating force upon its citizens would achieve the opposite of the proper purpose of a government; rather than protecting individual rights, the government would be abrogating them. This paradox cannot be evaded, and must therefore be addressed honestly, rejecting both mystical escape to legitimacy (social contract theory), or the outright denial of individual rights (collectivism).

How, then, could a government be financed without the violations of individual rights? There are many possibilities, but perhaps one of the best is one originated from Ayn Rand herself, in the form of contract enforcement fees (CEFs for short). In essence, a CEF is an optional fee that an agent can pay as a premium on a legal contract, which makes the specific contract legally binding and enforceable in a court of law. Agents would be free to opt out of the CEF, but doing so would make the contract legally unenforceable.

In addition to CEFs, a rights-respecting government could also enact a fee, permanent or temporary, on the exclusive ownership of intellectual property. Such an intellectual property enforcement fee (IPEF) would apply to patents and copyright, in exchange for the government's enforcement of the owner's exclusive production thereof. An IPEF is distinguished from a tax in that it is completely optional to pay without fear of forceful reprisal. In the refusal to pay such a fee, the government would cease to enforce such a patent or copyright. The originator of intellectual property would still be free to manufacture the product in question, but consequently would lose the *exclusive* right to produce it.

Another possibility is a premium, permanent or temporary, on the ability to vote in local or national elections. Since voting is not a negative right, but rather a privilege to partake in a specific legal process, such fees would be legitimate, so long as they are voluntary. Some may object to voting fees as creating risk for a rich aristocracy to form, but this wouldn't be an issue or danger so long as a government is constitutionally constrained properly. If the government isn't, direct democracy is arguably as great a danger to individual liberty as an aristocracy.

Finally, a rights-respecting government could enact a type of lottery, in which a certain proportion of the prize pool would be distributed to the winner(s). The purchase of such lottery tickets would be voluntary, but it would create an incentive for people to donate beyond the self-interest of being protected from crime.

All of these forms of financing also assume a complete void of voluntary donations to a government, even though it would be directly in one's own interests to do so. In a rational society, there would be a greater access understanding why the proper government services are necessary, and how they directly benefit every person. Additionally, lower taxes tend to increase the incentive for charitability all else being equal. A society completely devoid of taxation would have maximum incentive for charitability as opposed to any other possible society. If one wants evidence of the efficacy of voluntary government financing, one need only look at how much money people currently donate to voluntary charity, in which donors gain *nothing* in return. Voluntary government financing would give someone a huge benefit in return, in a very tangible way. Voluntary donations *alone* would be more than enough to pay for all necessary government services. The truth is that there are many ways to finance a government without resorting to coercion and oppression.

Allegations of Corruptibility

Some object to voluntary donations for government services on the grounds that they would create an increased incentive for corruption, and would over-represent high-paying donors. However, this is a false cause; corruption is possible whether or not a government is permitted to initiate force upon its citizens in the form of taxation. In reality, the incentive for corruption in a government is primarily determined by the strength of a government's constitution in preventing pressure-group warfare and political pull.

Some argue that if this were the case, wealthier people would have very little incentive to financially contribute to a government. However, those who are wealthier within a free enterprise society would have the most to lose financially if the government somehow went bankrupt. Those who are wealthier would also utilize more government services, such as contract enforcement and intellectual property enforcement, and would thus have a personal motivation to donate more to government services.

Social Contract Theory

Some may defend government taxation or inflation on the basis of social contract theory, which claims that taxation, is justified due to an alleged implicit agreement between the government and its citizens. According to social contract theory, there is nothing wrong with taxation, as such, since it simply represents commensurate payment for services, the same way that a business pays an employee, or a buyer pays a seller. But this claim is erroneous because individuals do not *consent* to receive such services, and thus do not consent to compensating the agency providing that service. Nor do individuals have the opportunity to evade such charges by relinquishing their use of the service in question. A restaurant, for instance, *can* forcibly charge its customers commensurate payment because its customers *chose* to use its goods/services. Additionally, its customers knew that they would have to pay for their food and service, and how much they would have to pay. Taxation, in contrast, is more comparable to extortion; individuals are forced to pay money without their consent, and regardless of whether they use a service (or good) in question under the threat of physical reprisal.

Social contract theory is a crude, dishonest, historical fabrication of a non-existent contract, agreed to by no one, completely boundless in scope, and legally inescapable. If a private business attempted to enforce such a "contract", what would be the response?

In this context the error in this reasoning is obvious. Advocates of social contract theory treat it as a mystically revealed, implicit agreement between the state and its citizens. However, as mentioned earlier in *Property*, contracts cannot be *imposed*; they have no legitimacy if not agreed to, and such a scheme of extortion cannot logically be considered a *contract*. Besides this, the "social contract" also has no defining limits, expiration, or enforcement because it is neither explicitly written nor spoken, and has no coherent conceptual framework whatsoever. According to social contract theory, the government cannot ever actually be wrong; everything that it does is magically consensual and justified, now matter how oppressive or tyrannical it is in reality. The "social contract" is a mystical, dishonest fabrication that has no legitimate basis in reality. The fact that many classical liberals, the so-called "defenders of capitalism" endorse this crude fiction is an appalling insult to the very concept of free enterprise.

Objections to Government

Because of the government's potential ability to destroy and dominate humans, many political philosophers conclude that there should be no government at all. Some alleged proponents of free enterprise, calling themselves Anarcho-capitalists or market anarchists, argue that all states are illegitimate because they necessarily eliminate competitors, thus initiating force and making the government a criminal apparatus. Anarcho-capitalism is the theoretical form of social organization, which lacks a centralized state, and protects individual and property rights instead via decentralized, private force wielders, which would allegedly "compete" with each other for the best laws and protection.

Political liberty requires a specific, objective code of laws; a code of laws precisely crafted for the protection of individual rights. Any agency attempting to "compete" with such a legal system, i.e. utilizing physical force in a manner contradictory to this code of laws becomes a criminal organization (insurrection) and must be forcefully suppressed. Even agencies allegedly tasked with "helping" the government by enforcing rights-protecting laws, and merely "competing" with it in fulfilling this task present an eminent threat to individual rights, due to the fact that such agencies (vigilantes) utilize physical force without the oversight and procedures of a government. If such an agency avoided this problem by subjecting itself to identical procedures and safeguards of a government, then that would be indistinguishable from *joining* it. Harry Binswanger brilliantly illustrates this point:

To carry out its function of protecting individual rights, the government must forcibly bar others from using force in ways that threaten the citizens' rights. Private force is force not authorized by the government, not validated by its procedural safeguards, and not subject to its supervision. **The government has to regard such private force as a threat—i.e., as a potential violation of individual rights**. In barring such private force, the government is retaliating against that threat [bolding added] (Binswanger).

In this connection, it is crucial to understand that the use of physical force is not a form of production, and thus cannot be put under competition. This would be a contradiction, because physical force neutralizes competition and makes production impossible. Agents using physical force, whether initiatory or retaliatory, justified or unjustified, are attempting to become monopolists. Physical force is not subject to negotiation, and does not adhere to the laws of supply and demand. Physical force is the *framework* from which all economic transactions are made possible or impossible. Harry Binswanger outlines this contradiction:

The most twisted evasion of the "libertarian" anarchists in this context is their view that disputes concerning rights could be settled by "competition" among private force-wielders on the "free market." This claim represents a staggering stolen concept: **there is no free market until after force has**

been excluded. Their approach cannot be applied even to a baseball game, where it would mean that the rules of the game will be defined by whoever wins it. This has not prevented the "libertarian" anarchists from speaking of "the market for liberty" (i.e., the market for the market) [bolding added] (Binswanger).

Harry Binswanger continues:

Production must be kept strictly separate from destruction. A business deals in the creation of goods and services to offer on a free market; a coercer deals in destruction. The proper use of destruction is to combat destruction-- to wield retaliatory force against the initiators of force. But retaliatory force is still destruction, not production. There is no such thing as "the market for force-wielding." **For there to be a market in the first place, those who would simply seize goods must be met with force.** The benefits of a free market presuppose freedom has been established. **Market mechanisms can't establish or protect the preconditions of there being a market** (Binswanger).

In effect, the Anarcho-capitalist approach to force would negate any possibility of an *actual* free market. If the United States became Anarcho-capitalist tomorrow, the result would simply be fragmentation into many smaller states, many of which would be likely to implement socialism or fascism, thus undermining any possibility of free enterprise in America. In fact, according to the Anarcho-capitalist view, we currently live under "market anarchy", as "the market" chose the United States government as its "defence agency". According to the Anarcho-capitalists, there is nothing that could possibly happen to stop "market anarchy" from prevailing. Even if the entire world was under the jurisdiction of one totalitarian state, such a scenario would be regarded as the "defence agency" chosen by "the market in force". Anarcho-capitalists argue that states would never be able to form under "market anarchy", since they extrapolate competition within free enterprise onto the use of force, and assume that it could never monopolize. Monopolies do not form in a free market *because* force has been extracted from society. This phenomenon does not apply to societies in "market anarchy" (civil war).

This view is completely unable to explain how state formation was even *possible* in the first place. Anarcho-capitalists accept two premises that together are incompatible with reality. The first is that it is impossible for states to form under market anarchy. The second is that there was a time on earth without any states. The conclusion of these two premises is that states, as such, are impossible. The fact that states currently exist alone is a sufficient refutation of the Anarcho-capitalist notion of "competition in force". As stated before, force is the thing that neutralizes competition. "Competition in force" is thus a contradiction in terms.

Government is the process of putting the use of retaliatory force under *objective* control; i.e. retaliatory force according to predictable, consistent, proper procedures. There cannot be multiple, mutually exclusive approaches to objectivity, and so there cannot be multiple, mutually exclusive approaches to individual rights. If two legal systems are mutually exclusive, then at least one of them is violating individual liberties. If there were hundreds or thousands of sets of mutually exclusive legal systems, the injustice perpetrated by them would be incalculable. Thus, a proper, rights-respecting government is the only possibility for individual liberty. In summary:

"Anarcho-capitalism" is a contradiction in terms. **Capitalism can exist only where rights are protected, including property rights. To protect rights, criminals who initiate force must be met with retaliatory force.** But the wielding of retaliatory force itself must be placed under objective control, by a constitutionally limited government with objective law. Otherwise, what results is not "competing defence agencies" but civil war. That war will be won by the gang with the most ruthless and most powerful army. Under anarchy, might, not right, determines what the "laws" will be (Binswanger).

Anarchy may appear to be the most consistent form of political freedom, but any notion of a "stateless" society kicks the metaphorical ladder out from underneath. Freedom requires an objective code of laws, which itself requires a constitutionally limited state. If freedom is to be maintained for any significant amount of time, agents cannot have the "freedom" to deprive others of liberty, and must be barred from doing so through retaliatory force.

Anarchy and free enterprise are opposites. Under anarchy, the initiation of physical force is permitted for all agents within it. Under free enterprise, the initiation of physical force is banned for all agents within it, including government agents. Free enterprise is a system of spontaneous order, in which agents within it are completely free from coercion, and have complete political freedom, never needing to fear physical reprisal unless they violate the rights of others. Anarchy is a system of chaos, in which its agents have no political freedom, and have to fear devastating force being unleashed against them at any moment. Thus, anarchy is the system most conducive to the proliferation of violence and tyranny, achieving the opposite of political liberty. It is only under free enterprise that rights are protected, and political liberty can be achieved. If you are an advocate of political freedom, then you must uphold free enterprise, and necessarily reject anarchism.

Chapter 4: Constitution

What specific restraints and limits should a government be bound by? In answering this question, it will be useful to analyse the United States Constitution, as the United States was arguably the closest society in history to ideal free enterprise. In this connection, it will be useful to appreciate where the United States Constitution succeeded in protecting individual liberties, and where it has been compromised or flawed, either by external pressure and attack, or by weak and improper language: by holes and vulgarities. Only the most important amendments (i.e. amendments most critical to the protection of individual liberties) will be analysed.

The First Amendment

The first amendment of the United States Constitution is the document protecting freedom of speech and expression, within both the commons (if any), and one's own property. In its words, the first amendment reads: "Congress shall make no law respecting an establishment of religion, or prohibiting the free exercise thereof; or abridging the freedom of speech, or of the press; or the right of the people peaceably to assemble, and to petition the Government for a redress of grievances" (United States Senate). In essence, the first amendment is a document preventing government imposition of speech restrictions onto private property or public property. However, it does not and was never meant to impose speech rules upon private enterprise, regardless of whether they are more or less restrictive of speech. This is a common misconception of free speech; understood properly in a political sense, it means that one cannot be censored by imposition from the state. Free speech does not mean the right to say whatever one wants to in all settings and contexts; a proper understanding of free speech is contingent upon a proper understanding of property, and its role in regulating speech. Speech restrictions are entirely legitimate as long as they are within the context of private property, but become illegitimate if imposed on someone else's property. For example, a private school may legitimately ban the use of swear words on its premises, for as long as that specific agency maintains ownership over that school. However, if a school attempts to forcefully dictate the use of profanity in all schools within its city, it becomes a criminal organization subject to punishment from the government. Thus, the difference between legitimate and illegitimate restrictions on speech becomes immediately clear.

If a private institution has a right to dictate speech on its own premises, does that mean that the government has the right to dictate speech on its premises? The government is an institution that is crucially different from that of all other types of organizations. Private enterprise, for example, has a completely voluntary relationship with all of its associated agents. No one is ever *forced* to go to a bank, farm, train station, etc. However, associated agents do *not* have this type of voluntary relationship with the government; properly so in some contexts. For example, no one can simply "choose" to be exempt from laws against murder, theft, assault, fraud, etc. Anything that the government does is backed by a monopoly on the use of physical force. Thus, any speech restriction policy that a government makes, even within the context of its own premises, is a legal declaration, in effect, that certain types of speech are criminal in all contexts, even if not contemporarily enforced. This is due to the fact, as mentioned before, that the government holds a legal *monopoly* on the use of physical force. Its policies are not humble preferences, but universal decrees, and thus it cannot have the right to dictate any speech, even on its own premises.

The first amendment is optimistically unique in that it has been impossibly difficult for its opponents to crack directly. Throughout the entire course of the United States' history, the first amendment of the Constitution has stood invincibly strong against impotent philosophical attack. Instead of attacking it directly, the opponents of free speech have needed to mask their intentions via the guise of "regulatory safety", and "common sense" political reform. Since all rights are integrated, the violation of some rights is logically and practically the violation of all other rights. As private companies become more regulated, with increased restrictions on what they can say and promote, their free speech is inevitably infringed upon. Economic activities cannot be fully separated from personal activities, and so it is conceptually incoherent to support both increased business regulation along with free speech.

A free enterprise society requires freedom of expression to exist, and cannot be maintained or preserved without its existence. The first amendment is arguably the most important amendment to the constitution for two reasons. The first is that free speech is very deeply connected and integrated to all other rights, as mentioned earlier. The second is that the first amendment protects the base of all individual rights: the right to one's own mind. A constitutional protection for freedom of expression is inescapably necessary for a free society.

The Second Amendment

The second amendment of the United States Constitution secures the right to keep and bear armaments for its citizens. In its words, the second amendment reads: "A well regulated Militia, being necessary to the security of a free State, the right of the people to keep and bear Arms, shall not be infringed" (United States Senate). The second amendment, in essence, protects the application of physical property rights to armaments. Approaching the second amendment from a proper egoist ethical and political base, it is clear that the second amendment is both completely legitimate and necessary to protect property rights.

Having said this, there are some types of annihilative (nuclear, chemical) armaments, which are too dangerous for ordinary citizens to wield, and thus must be subject to the legal safeguards of the state. Unlike conventional firearms, annihilative weapons cannot be utilized *without* violating individual rights; even if a nuclear warhead is detonated in a large desert or ocean, its fallout will still poison and kill many innocent people. Thus, a government must regard even the possession of such weapons as a threat to individual rights. It is because such weapons cannot be used without violating individual rights that the government is justified in seizing them by force.

The second amendment has become extremely contentious as of recent decades, as if physical property rights are somehow up for debate as soon as it comes to armaments. This arbitrary assertion is made without regard to basic principle, and its proponents do not appear to comprehend its totalitarian implications. The exact same reasoning could be applied to an array of goods including cars, knives, and baseball bats, as they can and have all been utilized to kill. Surely these goods should also be banned in order to protect the safety of innocent Americans. To create a mirror image of the leftists' "reasoning": clearly the opponents of the second amendment don't care about the approximately 41,000 innocent Americans killed in car accidents, the 1591 deaths from knives, and the 467 deaths from blunt objects in 2017 (National Safety Council) (Statista).

Then there is the genetic fallacy: the claim that because firearms are *designed* to kill, they are somehow qualitatively worse than cars, motorbikes, etc. But the intended design of a good does not determine how many people it will kill in reality. The truth is that some risk is inevitable, and that the legislator cannot prevent all forms of tragedy.

Another twisted evasion made by the opponents of the second amendment is their un-recognition that the United States already possesses gun control - to some degree. The second amendment has already been infringed upon via firearm regulations, bans, etc. and is continuously under attack by the opponents of free enterprise. Currently, the most powerful opponents of free enterprise, the modern left, are attempting to enlarge the constitutional breach slowly and gradually, and smash away America's last remnants of freedom.

Why then did the second amendment fail to completely endure the philosophical attacks against it? There are many reasons, but one of the most prominent is the common misunderstanding of its first half. It reads: "A well regulated Militia, being necessary to the security of a free State". This half of the second amendment should have been removed from the document entirely due to its vulgarities, risk of misinterpretation, and the fact that it justifies the legitimacy of physical property rights on the grounds that it is "necessary to the security of a free State". Many modern "liberals" misinterpret "A well regulated Militia" to mean that the second amendment condones the government imposing firearm regulations and restrictions, as if the founding fathers would create an amendment simultaneously preventing and enabling property rights violations. However, in this context, "regulated", meant the equivalent of "regular", or a part of everyday life. The founding fathers did not want such restrictions imposed upon a citizenry, which is why they *created* the amendment. However, even small holes and vulgarities in a document can create enormous opportunity for government agents to infringe upon civil liberties and physical property rights. The second half of the second amendment, on the other hand is incontestably precise. It reads: "the right of the people to keep and bear Arms, shall not be infringed". If this were the extent of the amendment, it would be so perfect that no philosophical attack could ever challenge it.

Contrary to what many proponents of the second amendment believe, the document is not nearly as effective at protecting individual liberty as they would hope. In order to save and restore America's freedom, the battle must be won with ideas, not bullets. A rifle is not an argument, and understanding does not flow from the muzzle of a gun. The document may be a last resort to complete tyranny, but it would cost lakes of blood. Additionally, the second amendment has also been completely ineffective at protecting any other amendments. Furthermore, any proponents of free enterprise must understand that the primary justification of the second amendment is not to uphold an insurrection, but to uphold an application of physical property rights.

The Fourth Amendment

The fourth amendment of the United States Constitution secures the right to privacy, and protects against unreasonable search and seizure. In its own words, the fourth amendment reads: "The right of the people to be secure in their persons, houses, papers, and effects, against unreasonable searches and seizures, shall not be violated, and no Warrants shall issue, but upon probable cause, supported by Oath or affirmation, and particularly describing the place to be searched, and the persons or things to be seized" (United States Senate). In essence, the fourth amendment protects two important rights: the right to the presumption of innocence (a derivative of the virtue of justice), and the right to privacy (a derivative of physical property rights). Unfortunately, the fourth amendment has been obliterated by the many oppressive responses to the September 11th terrorist attacks. The National Security Agency (NSA) has become an unconstitutional and illegitimate spy apparatus which violates the privacy of millions of innocent people by collecting their digital metadata without their consent, and which offers no compensation for this violation. It did not always commit such rights violations, but in 2001 in the aftermath of the September 11th attacks, the Patriot act allowed the United States Government to unilaterally spy on its citizens without any evidence or warrant (Congress). In one year, the fourth amendment of the constitution was incontestably annihilated. The issue, in this case, had nothing to do with the fourth amendment itself. The document itself is very well written, and clearly stood in opposition to the Patriot Act. Yet, the amendment crumbled without a defence, hearing, or consideration. Out of all amendments, it is the fourth that had the most tragic fate. It only took one terrorist attack to singlehandedly repeal it. Additionally, the Patriot Act has created enormous moral hazard for the NSA to act irresponsibly and carelessly with personal metadata. Predictably, this has lead to countless NSA scandals in which they were caught illegally colluding with *AT&T* in dragnet surveillance of ordinary Americans via domestic communications since the year the Patriot Act was instituted: 2001. In 2013, it was revealed that the NSA collected phone metadata, communications, etc. without probable cause or a warrant (Electronic Frontier Foundation). The NSA is an organization that commits crime on such a scale that its commonality has now become its defence.

A free society would require much more resilient protections against invasive government surveillance. A constitutional protection of this kind would need a more precise definition of what constitutes "unreasonable" search and seizure. It would also need more emphasis of the crime of both spying and surveillance. In the United States, however, this structure has all but collapsed.

The Fifth Amendment

The fifth amendment of the United States Constitution possesses a much wider scope than the previous three. In its own words, it reads: "No person shall be held to answer for a capital, or otherwise infamous crime, unless on a presentment or indictment of a Grand Jury, except in cases arising in the land or naval forces, or in the Militia, when in actual service in time of War or public danger; nor shall any person be subject for the same offence to be twice put in jeopardy of life or limb; nor shall be compelled in any criminal case to be a witness against himself, nor be deprived of life, liberty, or property, without due process of law; nor shall private property be taken for public use, without just compensation" (United States Senate). Similarly to the second amendment, the fifth amendment has been somewhat infringed upon, in its reference to double jeopardy. The fifth amendment reads: "nor shall any person be subject for the same offence to be twice put in jeopardy of life or limb;" Shockingly, there is one aspect in which double jeopardy was and is utilized by the United States Government: the enforcement of antitrust laws, such as the Sherman Antitrust Act of 1890. Allegedly put in place to prevent monopolies, antitrust laws put restrictions on "unfair competition practices". In practice, this means that if a business sells a good or service at a price "too low", then that business is guilty of "predatory pricing", and is engaging in "exclusionary tactics" against competitors. Thus, that business is guilty of antitrust. If a business sells their product at a price equal to that of their competitors, then they are guilty of "collusion", and are again guilty of antitrust. If a business sells a good or service at a price "too high", then they are engaging in "price fixing", and are once again guilty of antitrust. Since there is no objective definition of what constitutes "predatory pricing", "collusion", or "price fixing", antitrust laws essentially criminalize all business activities, since there is no way for a private enterprise to be certain of its innocence or guilt of antitrust. Their innocence or guilt of antitrust cannot be predicted before determining a price at which to sell their good or service. Furthermore, a business's punishment or acquittal of antitrust is never determined by an objective criterion; only by whim. Additionally, there is no limit to how many times a business can be punished for being guilty of antitrust for as long as it keeps operating. If a business is found guilty of antitrust, and a particular judge enforcing the law is determined to keep punishing that business via "trust-busting" then that business will have to either keep risking punishment, or go out of business entirely. It is thus that antitrust has been utilized as a political tool for particular politicians to persecute particular disfavoured businesses. How exactly this is supposed to prevent monopolies from forming is inconceivable.

If antitrust laws are meant to be at least somewhat objective, then one possible solution to this problem would be to use the contemporary equilibrium price on a good or service as being the "fair price" for sale and purchase (although even that would be constantly in flux, and somewhat unpredictable). The government could then use approximately three standard deviations higher or lower from the equilibrium price as the standards for "predatory pricing" and "price fixing", respectively. Even if "predatory pricing" and "price fixing" were defined as being as restrictive as one standard deviation higher or lower from the equilibrium price, it would still be better than the rule of unreason enforced today. Such a compromise would still be illegitimate; the government has no "right" to punish businesses for the sale of a good or service, regardless of price. Criminalizing trade, outside the context of aiding a rights-violator, is still a form of tyranny.

Another way in which the Fifth Amendment creates hazard for individual liberty is in its concluding sentence. It reads: "nor shall private property be taken for public use, without just compensation". Unlike many other flaws in the United States Constitution, this part of the amendment is not merely a misuse of language. It is a critical error, and one that has resulted in mass property rights violations all across America. In essence, it allows the government to seize any amount of property by force from its rightful owner, in exchange for its undefined "just compensation". This aspect of the amendment, being the basis for eminent domain laws, is incredibly hazardous not just in its capacity to result in never-ending rights violations, but also in its capacity to distort the impartial forces of the market and to incentivize corruption and political pull. Eminent domain can be used to erect aggressive barriers to competition in a certain field of goods/services. If, for example, a rich political donor owns a supermarket company, and seeks to eliminate his competition to establish a monopoly, he can influence the mayor of a town to "coincidentally" enact an eminent domain seizure against the donor's competitors' stores. Their land would then be turned into places for public/civic use, and the donor would enjoy a monopoly on supermarkets within the town, and could shoot down competitors with impunity. Additionally, eminent domain laws can create moral hazard for failing businesses and allow them to escape the negative consequences of their actions. If, for example, the owner of a farm fails to maintain his crops properly, causing them to die, he can escape his mal-investment if his farm is seized from him in exchange for money. The money used to compensate the victims of such expropriation is always gained through the criminal process of taxation, or through the fraudulent theft of inflation. Finally, eminent domain laws also create an incentive for politicians to be wrathful and vindictive to their political, social, or personal opposition. If solely one person or group heavily criticizes a politician, and that politician wields the power of eminent domain, then that politician could "coincidentally" seize that person or group's homes, for "civic" use, and leave them homeless. Eminent domain incentivizes corrupt, irresponsible, morally hazardous behaviour. As mentioned before in the analysis of the first amendment, all rights are integrated. Eminent domain is just another example of how an infringement upon property rights is also an infringement upon freedom of speech and expression.

The United States Constitution, being an imperfect document, possesses many holes and vulgarities, which have caused it to be abused, twisted, and infringed upon outright. Despite this, the United States has managed to endure over 200 years of philosophical assault, and is still relatively high on the freedom scale even today. The constitution of the government of an ideal free enterprise society would not possess such errors; so one would expect it to be even more stable and free. But which constitutional protections did the United States Constitution miss that are critically important to the protection of individual rights?

Constitutional Omissions

The United States Constitution includes rather weak protections for intellectual property, and bases it on an improper justification. It reads: "To promote the Progress of Science and useful Arts by securing for limited

Times to Authors and Inventors the exclusive Right to their respective Writings and Discoveries;" (United States Senate). There are multiple errors in this protection, the first being its justification for intellectual property rights. This protection implies that intellectual property is only justified "To promote the Progress of Science and useful Arts", and mentions no *moral* right for its originator to have the exclusive right to the product of his/her own mind. In reality, the value of a specific intellectual enterprise is completely irrelevant to the legitimacy of that enterprise. It is true that strong intellectual property protections *do* help the "Progress of Science and useful Arts", but this is merely a derivative issue. Is the aim of this declaration really to justify intellectual property rights based on how effectively it can serve other people *besides* the originator? What about the right of an individual to the product of one's mind?

This protection aims to achieve the "securing for limited Times... the exclusive Right to... [intellectual property]". How much time? One lifetime? Decade? Year? Month? Week? This language again is open to abuse, and provides likely insufficient protections for intellectual property. Finally, this protection mentions "the exclusive Right to their... Discoveries". As mentioned earlier, a discovery cannot be a legitimate form of intellectual property, since its existence is *not* contingent upon the discoverer. By mentioning discoveries, this protection undermines the legitimacy of all intellectual property rights. In addition to all these criticisms, this constitutional protection should also have mentioned the creators of *all* types of intellectual property; of who's intellectual property's legitimacy is to be determined by the standard mentioned earlier in *Property*. Because only certain types of intellectual property creators were mentioned, there are currently extremely weak protections for intellectual property creators and inventors in regards to digital and Internet content. Many digital and internet content creators currently have to beg their audiences for online donations, using tools like GoFundMe and Patreon, rather than being able to sell their products as if they was any other type of consumer product. This abject self-abasement and appeasement is the inevitable consequence of the insufficient protection of rights.

The United States Constitution also lacks protections against irrational and whimsical laws; i.e. laws without any objective definition, application, punishment, etc. and solely determined by subjective whim. That is the cause of, under the guise of "saving" free enterprise, the antitrust laws, which have actually done the most to mutilate, distort, and destroy it. As mentioned earlier, antitrust laws, in effect, *criminalized* all private sales of goods and services within the United States of America. Antitrust has been selectively enforced, but the power exists to persecute and destroy regardless. Irrational, whimsical law can lead to nothing but destruction, and so a constitutional protection against it is incalculably important. The only thing standing in between rational beings and enslavement is the existence of *objective law*. Without it, no freedom is possible, and civilization is doomed to perish.

Chapter 5: Warfare

Warfare is an unfortunate reality of the modern and historical world. Wars can be fought over resources, religion, ideology, race, etc. but they are enabled and perpetrated by authoritarian governments and social systems. The more authoritarian a society becomes, the greater the need and incentive to invade other nations. As fascistic governments restrict trade and commerce, they become more reliant on plundering and looting as a means of sustenance and survival. As the rational means of survival are taken away from agents (trade and production), they have to rely on the irrational means of survival (invasion and plunder). This is why it has been the most fascistic, authoritarian states that have historically been responsible for invasions and wars: Nazi Germany, Soviet Russia, Imperial Japan, Fascist Italy, etc.

Incentives For War

Free enterprise societies, in contrast, have the minimum incentive for war; trade does not proliferate on a battlefield, and factories do not function under bombardment. Since free enterprise has the least incentive for political pull and corruption between businesses and the government, businessmen tend to be extremely averse to going to war with other nations. Rather, they have an interest in maintaining peace. If the government goes to war with other states, businessmen lose out on countless potential customers, investors, associates, employees, etc. from those nations, and thus lose out on potential profits via opportunity cost.

Since the government in a fully free enterprise society is financed voluntarily, it would have incredible difficulty financing an unprovoked invasion of a foreign society. If the government attempted to do this within a free enterprise society, its unpopularity would result in a massive reduction in government revenues, thus crippling the government's ability to launch such an invasion. If, however, a foreign invader attacked a free enterprise society, the government would be incredibly able and equipped to defend and retaliate against it. Since a free enterprise society is the system most conducive to the generation of wealth, the government would have a handsome abundance of money to finance its defensive capabilities via donations. Additionally, a free enterprise society would have the maximum incentive for innovation in armaments and defensive goods due to its strong intellectual property protections, lack of regulations, etc. out of all possible social systems. It would thus have the most advanced and effective equipment, weaponry, etc. to defend itself from a foreign invader all else being equal. Finally, a foreign invader would not just have to contend with the military of a free enterprise society; since the right to bear arms would be instantiated in its constitution (including more advanced weaponry than the United States currently allows), an invader would *still* have to contend with a well-armed militia of citizens even *if* it were able to rival the defensive military capacities of a free enterprise society (which is incredibly dubious).

Just War Theory

Nearly all political perspectives believe that warfare can be justified under certain conditions. According to Objectivism, war is only justified when it is used in retaliation against the violators of rights; in order to protect rights, a government must be able to crush foreign attackers. It is important to note that pre-emptive strikes upon probable cause can be justified according to Objectivism, as they constitute retaliation against a threat to individual rights. It is also justified for a government to invade societies, which are *essentially* tyrannical, not free; this constitutes retaliation against violations of the citizens' rights. Note that the term "justified" in this context means only that a particular country has no right to self-determination for as long as it remains essentially un-free. This does not necessarily tell a free society whether it *should* invade an un-free society; under most circumstances it is too selflessly generous to risk the lives of a nation's' citizens in order to establish freedom for others.

If a free society goes to war, its goal is to crush the enemy as quickly and decisively as possible, and must be prepared use it most powerful and destructive armaments in order to defeat the enemy. A free society cannot half-fight in such a conflict; it must use whatever means in its disposal to protect its citizens' rights, including those, which are likely to cause casualties of innocents on the opposing side. During a period of wartime, a government cannot afford to use merely proportionate punishment; this is only possible when a government has legal jurisdiction in an area. It must fight at its best and most effective capabilities in order to gain a complete surrender against the opposing side. Anything else is insufficient to be called a "victory"; it would only be a prolonged stalemate.

Conscription

Under no circumstances would a proper government ever be permitted to conscript soldiers for offensive or defensive purposes. Conscription is one of the most brutal violations of individual rights ever perpetrated by governments historically and presently. Furthermore, it negates the most fundamental individual right: the right to life. It affirms that an individual does not have a right to live out and dispose of his own life, and that his death in service to others can be forced upon him: pure altruism. This morally cannibalistic violation has enabled one of the worst military disasters in the history of the United States: the Vietnam War. The Vietnam War was the perfect representation of the real, unmasked purpose of conscription, not its *alleged* purpose. The purpose of conscription is *invasion*, not last-resort defence, as many "conservatives" allege. If a foreign invader ever attacked a free enterprise society, it would have an abundance of volunteer soldiers. As with all other moral issues, the false dichotomy of "the moral *versus* the practical" doesn't hold up. The moral *is* the practical. Volunteer armies are more effective than conscript armies all else being equal. James Pattison explains the flaws of conscript armies:

The effectiveness of a conscripted force, however, is open to question. A short term of duty means conscripts cannot be trained properly, which is particularly a concern in more complex military operations. A longer term of duty may allow for greater training, but will reduce the number of those drafted overall, which impacts on the case for tackling the civil-military gap, and, given that it is longer, significantly undermines individual autonomy. In addition, a system of universal or random conscription can be expected to conscript many individuals unsuited to performing military operations effectively (Pattison).

Conscript armies, because of their lack of choice, tend to be apathetic about fighting. They will attempt to protect themselves, but they have no ideal or value to fight for. Thus, there is very little motivation, besides basic survival, for a conscript to go above and beyond in their service. Additionally, conscript soldiers tend to quit the military as soon as they are legally allowed to, making them only short-term agents in the military.

Volunteer armies, in contrast, have potent motivation to fight for their ideals. They will exert much more effort, initiative, etc. in order to defeat an invader, and will, if anyone, be the soldiers willing to go above and beyond what is expected or required of them. A volunteer soldier is a soldier with conviction, tenacity and will fight to the death for his cause. James Pattison articulates the advantages of volunteer armies:

The effectiveness of the all-volunteer force (AVF) is one of its greatest benefits. A standing, professional army provides the possibility of extensive training and integration: these enhance flexibility since soldiers can prepare for a variety of potential conflicts. It has been argued that the AVF is effective as, first, the recruits perform better because they volunteer; and, second, it can select well-qualified recruits, which means that its recruits are more easily trained and present fewer disciplinary problems (Pattison).

Free enterprise capitalism, out of all social systems, has the least incentive for war. However, if attacked, it would still be ready and able to defend itself in a manner superior to its invader all else being equal. This does not mean that a free enterprise society is impossible to conquer, only that for any *given* society, free enterprise has the highest likelihood of being able to repel an invasion out of all social systems.

Part Two: Practice

Chapter 6: The Economy

Free enterprise is the social system, which upholds the complete separation of state and the economy; it does *not* imply a mixed economy, in which the government plays an active and interventionist role in the domain of businesses and enterprises. Government is not responsible for dictating prices, wages, licensing, production, etc. of private enterprise. The only role of the government in such a system is to protect individual liberties, and property rights (intellectual or otherwise), by punishing instances of criminal behaviour whenever they occur. Note that the term "criminal" in this context means "a violator of individual rights". A common error in economics and law is to conflate actual criminals with whomever the government decrees to be a *de jure* lawbreaker. In a proper free enterprise system, there would be no legal difference between the two. A system of free enterprise, otherwise known as laissez-faire capitalism, permits no breach upon property rights by the government except as punishment for a rights violation.

As stated before, within free enterprise all economic activities including production, distribution, and trade are all subject to *private* ownership. In essence, private ownership entails the *exclusion* of at least one person(s) in legal possession and use of a certain good. In practical, everyday life, private property is much more exclusive than this definition, usually being under the exclusive possession and use of one or more person(s). Theoretically, any given property owner could *choose* to allow anyone and everyone to have equal access to their property, thus making it *universally*, not *privately* owned. However, this would likely never happen under free enterprise due to the enormous moral hazard created by such an ownership system. Various property owners *may* choose to create a mutualistic enterprise, syndicalist cooperative, etc., but this would *only* be possible under a free enterprise legal system. This would not be possible in a totalitarian, centrally planned economy, only a decentralized free enterprise economy. Furthermore, such cooperatively owned enterprises would likely be in the minority, not majority. It is more likely that more exclusive corporate enterprises would become popular instead.

In regard to corporations, many opponents of free enterprise argue that monopolies and collusion are the products of a free, unregulated market. This claim is not only false, but the complete opposite of the truth. In reality, free enterprise actually tends to subvert and undercut potential monopolies due to its coercion-free environment. As the initiation of physical force is banned from human relationships, it becomes impossible to suppress competitors within any field or industry.

Monopolies

For reference, a monopoly is not just a state of affairs in which a business has no *active* competition, but a state of affairs in which competition with a given business is made to be *impossible*. This can only be done through the erection of aggressive barriers against would-be competitors. Many policies allegedly designed to protect "consumer safety", or "the little guy" makes monopolistic scenarios more likely, including occupational licensing, subsidies, tariffs, bailouts, and quotas. These policies, being antithetical to free enterprise, increase the difficulty for competitors to emerge, profit once they emerge, or provide an unfair advantage to some companies over others. Opponents of free enterprise argue that large businesses could buy up all of its competitors, thereby cornering market on a good or service. However, small businesses are just as strategic as aspiring monopolists. Attempting to buy out all your competitors will result in them charging exceptionally high prices for their business. Throughout this endeavour, competitors will be much more efficient than the aspiring monopolist all else being equal because of their greater capacity for capital investment, thereby undercutting the bloated giant. If, somehow, a business is able to buy off all of the given competitors in a given field it would have no way of stopping competitors emerging at any moment. Predatory pricing may be able to stop some competitors, but it is ultimately unsustainable for a business to utilize.

Collusion

Collusion fails in free enterprise for very similar reasons to monopolies. Collusion plans by their nature in a dynamic economy are impractical and run into many logistical issues even before their implementation. Associates within collusion would need to determine exactly what price at which to sell their good or service. Setting equal prices for products or services with differing levels of quality and manufacturing costs would give disproportionate advantage to certain businesses in the collusion. This would financially incentivize the least advantaged businesses within the collusion to turn against it. Prices determined proportional to quality and manufacturing costs would incentivize the majority of the population to buy the cheaper good or service, thus producing uneven sales and benefit to certain businesses in the collusion over others. Given that it would be more financially profitable to turn against the collusion, it would be incentivized to all competitors within it. The businesses choosing to turn against the collusion would attract the overwhelming majority of sales, and would thus become much more successful than its competitors. Without the use of physical force, one cannot stop others from engaging in profitable activities.

Wage Labour

Many opponents of free enterprise argue against the very notion of trading labour in exchange for capital in a state of being in which the labourer does not own industry. This process, known as wage labour, is an integral part of free enterprise. It allows those without ownership of industry to achieve economic sustenance, and has resulted in the enrichment of billions of people.

Exploitation

Wage labour is accused of being "exploitative", since an employer gains a profit from the agreement. In this exchange, the employer's economic gain in production from the labourer is greater than the costs of paying the labourer. Critics of free enterprise conclude that such a relationship is inherently unjust, and must be overturned partially or completely. The more moderate critics of this relationship advocate for minimum wage laws in order to force wages at or above the market equilibrium (which always results in unintended consequences). Seeing that this is only pushing the problem back a step, the extreme critics of wage labour conclude that workers or the government should use physical force to seize industry from its owner, in order to collectivize it. Notice that the critics of wage labour regard "exploitation" as being morally unacceptable, but hold no qualms about advocating for (and perhaps participating in) an industrial class war.

The critics of wage labour miss the fact that the "exploitative" relationship between labourers and employers is actually mutual. To the employer, the money spent on paying labourers is worth less than the employer's gain in productivity from the labour. However, to the labourer, the money gained from the exertion of labour is worth more than the work itself. Economics is *not* a zero-sum game. Since values are relational, no party necessarily has to lose in any economic transaction. Within free enterprise, all rationally self-interested transactions are *mutually* beneficial.

Labour Unions

There is nothing about the concept or implementation of a labour union that is in any sense antithetical to the principles of free enterprise. In a free, competitive society, a labour union is merely a voluntary association of employees who, together, bargain for higher wages. In doing so, unions do not violate personal or property rights, so long as they are not permitted to force others to join their ranks. Government measures alleged to be "crushing unions", such as right to work laws are merely the relinquishment of union coercion by allowing workers to freely associate and disassociate with unions as they choose. The government cannot legitimately suppress individuals from associating with a union, but it must suppress a union's attempt to force others into it. The government should be an impartial rights-protecting agency, rather than an agency tasked with enforcing the whims of any socio-economic group.

Labour unions, while legitimate in principle, are often alleged to be a much more consequential force than what their track records suggest. Many advocates of labour unions act as if unions somehow raise the standard of living for all participants within them, regardless of context. Labour unions can be useful apparatuses in certain contexts; if industry moves into a newly developing town such that there is a temporary lack of active competition, a labour union can raise wages to the equilibrium level. However, apart from exceptional circumstances, wages tend to be extremely elastic within free enterprise. Wages are determined by a process of supply and demand via labourers competing for employers and vice versa, *not* by an employer's whim. High wages are not necessarily indicative of an employer's benevolence, and low wages are not necessarily indicative of an employer's unscrupulousness. Labourers are not slaves, and thus have multiple possible options for employment. This results in the employer, not just labourers, being faced with competition. The employer's wages need to be near-equilibrium in order to expect anyone to work for the business.

Child Labour

Critics of wage labour, to denounce free enterprise, cite the industrial revolution, in which children had to labour in factories in order to achieve sustenance. The critics of wage labour predictably drop its historical context, comparing it to the modern-day living conditions of the United States as evidence of the "evils of capitalism", and the "necessity" of economic restrictions and controls. Critics of wage labour evade the fact that child labour was prevalent throughout human history before the industrial revolution. They also evade the fact that it was only through the process of industrialization that child labour could be discontinued. The United States only passed laws prohibiting child labour *because* there was barely any child labour left. The first U.S national legislation restricting child labour was passed in 1938 by F.D.R during the great depression, well after the end of the industrial revolution. If the United States federal government passed laws prohibiting child labour during industrialization, the only options left would be a) to discontinue child labour and thereby let children starve to death, or b) to transfer child labour into the black market. But since child labour was already on the decline during and after the industrial revolution, it must have been the rising living standards and prosperity of this period that allowed more children to go to school instead of working in factories. The generation of wealth is the only thing that can ever end child labour, not government restrictions or controls.

The Nature of Money

Money, put simply, is an abstraction of economic value. It is a form of wealth that is designed to have liquidity; i.e. the ability to be transmuted into the equivalent a vast number of possible combinations of goods or services. The purpose of money within an economy is twofold: to give each individual who uses it an increased range of economic choice unachievable in a barter society, and to allow each individual more economic security against unpredictable events and contingencies. Money tends to spontaneously emerge from barter societies as an inevitable result of its requirement in the economy. It makes economic trade incredibly easy, because it allows traders to avoid the risk of not having the specific appropriate good/service to trade for another specific good/service.

Price Systems

Another advantage of money is its consequence of creating universal, impartial price systems, which allow one to estimate the approximate objective value of goods/services to an extent otherwise impossible. Decentralized price systems are also advantageous in that they can avoid the famous economic calculation problem discovered by Ludwig Von Mises. Suppose a socialist central planner is tasked with the manufacturing and distribution of lightbulbs for the city of Moscow. How could this central planner determine how many lightbulbs should be manufactured? A central planner could not simply estimate two or three lightbulbs for each home, since there are many buildings, such as factories and hospitals, which require many more lightbulbs. However, there are also many homes and buildings which cannot utilize lightbulbs, because they aren't connected to electricity networks. How, then, is this number of lightbulbs to be determined? If the socialist central planner orders the production and distribution of too many lightbulbs, then the labour and materials to manufacture them will go to waste, as they could have been employed for more useful purposes. However, if the central planner orders the manufacturing and distribution of too few lightbulbs, then there will be many homes without proper lighting in Moscow for many days, weeks, or months, and the manufacturing of such lightbulbs would be slow and inefficient, which again would waste time. In a free enterprise system, the solution to this problem is simple: keep manufacturing and selling lightbulbs as long as it is profitable to do so. If it is cheaper to manufacture the lightbulbs than it is to sell them, then a business should keep manufacturing and selling lightbulbs. Thus, a decentralized pricing system is able to effectively and impartially align the interests of a business with the interests of wider society. Furthermore, a decentralized pricing system is immune to the bias and human error prevalent in a system of central economic planning.

The Proper Currency

A proper currency is one that is tied to the value of a scarce physical resource; preferably a resource that is exceptionally valuable in comparison to other resources. Money must also be homogeneous, divisible, durable, verifiable, transportable, and must be a stable store of value. The more commensurate a medium of money is with these characteristics, the more effective it is as a form of liquid currency. Gold and silver make excellent basis for a currency; they both possess objective *aesthetic* value, and both align with the characteristics listed above. Crude oil can also be used as a basis for currency, but can suffer from price instability, especially as fossil fuels are gradually replaced by green technologies. Because a proper currency possesses an objectively verifiable value, it tends to be very stable and secure against unpredictable and unforeseeable contingencies such as economic hardship, nationwide conflict, etc. Additionally, it requires no central issuer, and is therefore immune to the pernicious phenomenon of inflation found in fiat currencies.

Fiat Currency

Unlike proper forms of currency, fiat currency presents many hazardous injustices perpetrated with full knowledge of their immorality. The United States Constitution contains no defence against a hazardous, government imposed system of fiat currency, which incentivizes manipulation, corruption, and theft. Shockingly, the United States Constitution includes a measure which allows the government "To coin Money, regulate the Value thereof, and of foreign Coin, and fix the Standard of Weights and Measures;", and "To provide for the Punishment of counterfeiting the Securities and current Coin of the United States;". Government imposed fiat currency systems are hazardous not only because they make legalized counterfeiting via "inflation" virtually inevitable, but also because the value of a fiat currency is completely contingent on what people *believe* the value of the currency is, making it hazardous and unstable. Fiat currency is extremely vulnerable to spontaneous cascades of panic caused by internal conflict, external hostility, nationwide mal-investment, etc. leading to massive reductions in the value of fiat currency, and thus massive economic loss for the nations' citizens. Fiat currencies are also highly vulnerable to unilateral manipulation, making them unreliable and poor stores of value. Due to these two factors, fiat currencies disincentivize investment and lead to an increase in time preference all else being equal. As time preference increases, individuals are incentivized to make decisions that favour short-term gains over long-term gains, and thus such a scenario incentivizes people to act against their own rational self-interest. Individuals are more incentivized to spend money, as the value of the currency constantly decreases, even if their spending is irresponsible or useless. Thus, fiat currencies also distort market demand, disproportionately over-representing demand for short term goods/services, and disproportionately under-representing demand for long term goods/services.

Cryptocurrencies

Due to the pernicious effects and incentives created by fiat currencies, many proponents of free enterprise are desperate to look for alternatives. One such alternative is a form of digital technology known as "block-chain", which serves as the base for a type of digital currency and digital asset known as cryptocurrencies. Cryptocurrencies, akin to currencies with the backing of a scarce good, requires no central issuer; they function using a completely decentralized network capable of processing transactions with incalculable precision.

Many proponents of free enterprise favour cryptocurrencies because they are immune to the phenomenon of inflation; they have no central issuer, and units of such a currency only come into existence whenever a certain type of code has been discovered by a computer (the phenomenon of "mining"). However, there are established limits on how many units of any given cryptocurrencies can exist, which is delimited by the specific programmer(s) of that currency.

Cryptocurrency is a temporary workaround - not an ideal solution - to fiat currencies, as they currently exist. A proper currency would be backed by the objective value of a scarce resource; preferably that of a luxury, non-perishable metal such as gold or silver. Both gold and silver have objectively valuable application; gold can be used as a component of digital devices, made into spacesuits, and both gold and silver can be crafted into jewellery. These functions make these currencies much more secure against unforeseeable events and contingencies, since they do possess objective

economic value. But cryptocurrencies still suffer from a very similar problem

as fiat currencies; their shared lacking of *objective* value. The value of both

cryptocurrencies and fiat currencies are determined by what people are

willing to trade in exchange for them. In other words, the value of both fiat

currency and cryptocurrency are exactly equivalent to what people *believe*

their values to be. Thus, cryptocurrencies are not entirely equipped for the

task of replacing fiat currencies and the many hazards that emerge thereof.

However, they are a step in the right direction, and are clearly preferable to

the type of money in popular circulation.

The Nature of Banking

Banking is the process of providing two opposite services in regards

to money: lending, and saving. A bank is an institution that borrows money

from investors before lending that money away at a higher rate of interest.

Banks fulfil two important functions within the economy. The first is that

they allow investors to gain a secure investment on their excess liquid capital.

The second is that they introduce more capital into the economy through

lending, and enable more business ventures, entrepreneurship, etc. to become

possible. Essentially, banks prevent the flow of capital from becoming static within an economy; they enable liquid capital itself to be a dynamic resource available for its most *objectively* valuable application.

Free Enterprise vs. Central Banking Systems

This aforementioned phenomenon, however, is only possible in a decentralized, free banking system. If a central bank is instituted into an economy, interest rates are determined not by the forces of supply and demand within a decentralized price system, but rather by fiat; by estimation. Central banks create many economic hazards that would otherwise be avoided by a free enterprise banking system. Firstly, interest rates as determined by central banks are incredibly vulnerable to human error; they simply cannot match the sheer precision of supply and demand based interest rates. A central bank's interest rate policies cannot spontaneously self-correct, as is possible in a decentralized banking system. If a central bank makes interest rates too low, it will cause a disproportionate incentive for borrowing money, thus leading to the establishment of hazardous business ventures. These mal-investments will not be immediately obvious; it requires time for them to fail, making apparent the critical mistakes of the central bank. It will be, at this point, too late for the central bank to correct its error; the economic damage would have already been done. The central bank's only viable medium to long term strategy at this point would be to dramatically raise interest rates, causing the most recent mal-investors to become bankrupt. However, if the central bank does not pull the plug on its interest rate policies, it will incentivize further and further mal-investment, which is economically unsustainable and disastrous. Likewise, if a central bank makes interest rates too high, it will result in a decreased incentive for borrowing. This will result in a slowing of economic expansion. An economy operating on this level of interest rates will lose out on potential productivity and efficiency via opportunity cost.

If interest rates are too low in a decentralized banking system, the issue would be automatically corrected via supply and demand. Interest rates that are too low would result in a decreased incentive to lend out money, and an increased incentive to borrow. There would then be a disproportionately great number of borrowers and small number of lenders. As the scarcity of money lending becomes more severe, this would result in more competition amongst borrowers, causing interest rates to increase, until they meet the equilibrium level. Likewise, if interest rates were too high in a decentralized banking system, this phenomenon would be resolved via a mirror image of the previously described process: an overabundance of lenders and scarcity of borrowers would cause an increase in competition amongst the lenders to satisfy the borrowers, thus leading to a decrease in interest rates back to the equilibrium level. A free market banking system is a decentralized, dynamic network. It is equipped with automatic stabilizers absent to a central bank, and is much less prone to error.

Depressions

Historically and presently, free enterprise has been accused of being responsible for inevitable periodic economic depressions. Allegedly, if an economy is left unregulated and uncontrolled, its prices, interest rates, and production will become sporadic, chaotic, and unpredictable. The opponents of free enterprise associate this phenomenon with The Great Depression of the 1930's and The Global Financial Crisis of 2008. However, the cause of these disasters was the opposite free market: the centralized banking system known as the Federal Reserve.

It is important to recognize, in this connection, that a free enterprise economic system does have periodic *recessions*, but not *depressions*. A recession is a temporary economic readjustment, in which a small part of the economy must slow production in order to adapt to new economic circumstances. Thus, a recession is a healthy economic process which purges excess, preventing individuals and businesses from succumbing to mal-investment and bankruptcy on a wide scale. A depression, in contrast, is a large-scale or nationwide slow in economic activity, in which certain industries and sectors of the economy suffer severe mal-investment and loss of economic value. Thus, a depression is the result of a recession not being allowed to occur properly. The result is impoverishment on a colossal scale and over a prolonged period of time.

Depressions are not part of the business cycle, nor are they an inevitable product of an unregulated market; the only thing capable of bringing such economic ruination is an institution able to *force* the economic error into existence; by monopolizing the rate of interest on all borrowing within the economy, central banks have a tendency to lower interest rates below a sustainable level. After the mal-investment has occurred and manifested itself, only the symptoms of depressions are immediately visible, but the cause remains hidden. After the manifestation of a depression, businessmen are blamed for getting "drunk", but no one bats an eye at the metaphorical bartender: the central bank. Through the misidentification of the central cause of depressions, a vicious cycle manifests itself: (1) State economic interventionism creates impoverishment. (2) The free market is blamed for said impoverishment. (3) Increased state interventionism into the economy is instituted. (4) Repeat steps 1-3. As this process continues, the poison that causes economic ruination is perceived as a divine balm. The screaming and wailing about the alleged "evils" of capitalism become louder as the true mechanics of the free market become more abrogated, mutilated, and destroyed.

Automation

It is commonly believed that, due to the effects of automation, an eminent jobless future awaits us. According to this theory, humans will inevitably become obsolete in every area of production, as machines will become superior in every endeavour. Thus, a system of voluntary exchange featuring wage labour too becomes obsolete. Proponents of this theory conclude either that a system of universal basic income (UBI), or the complete abolition of private property will become necessary.

What does this theory take for granted about the nature of employment? Firstly, it assumes that employment is a static, limited quantity, of which constantly decreases throughout history. But this argument collapses the moment one begins to concretize such a phenomenon from a historical perspective. One century ago, there was no such thing as a software engineer, radio host, television producer, movie actor, computer programmer, etc. Countless new jobs came into existence thanks to the development and improvement of technology. It is true that the horse and buggy industry became obsolete, but the automobile industry came to take its place. Likewise, labour-saving technologies continue to liberate man's time, allowing him to engage in other productive ventures. As humans move into the digital age, many individuals are now able to complete tasks never before thought possible, and with unparalleled efficiency.

Proponents of the jobless future theory argue that there is an inherent limit to the productive ventures human beings can engage in. Many individuals cite the immutable limit of natural resources in the universe as a justification for this notion. But this argument evades the fact that there is no limit to how much *wealth* can be produced using scarce goods. Utilizing only one canvas and an array of different paint colours, Leonardo Da Vinci's *Mona Lisa* holds incredible *aesthetic* value to human beings. But the materials, which compose the Mona Lisa on their own, are hardly worth a fraction of the painting's total value. Any limit on productive ventures humans can engage in is determined by the amount of wealth that can be produced from such ventures. But since there is no inherent limit to how much wealth can be produced from scarce physical resources, productive ventures are only limited by man's *imagination*.

Some may argue that even man's imagination and creativity will inevitably be surpassed by a superior artificial intelligence. Even if this is true, there are still certain types of employment, which will survive even the most extreme future of automation. Those ventures which provide a uniquely *human* experience, i.e. actors, performers, athletes, artists etc. will become the future of employment.

Part of the value of many ventures *is* the fact that humans achieve them. If a robot were able to create a carbon copy of the *Mona Lisa*, would this be able to parallel the value of the real thing? No; part of the value of such a craft is the *creator*. As Ayn Rand discovered, art represents a concretization of an artist's metaphysical value judgements; it is a projection of that artist's sense of life. Thus, a piece of art only has value if it is representative of the artist. As with many other creative ventures, part of the value is lost when a machine replaces it.

There is no inherent limit to the productive capacity of human beings, and so there is no inherent limit to how fulfilling human life can be. There is no conceivable point at which human life becomes "too good". Employment will not be the same in the future as it is today, but it is in so sense a dying practice.

Chapter 7: Healthcare

Healthcare is arguably the most important combination of goods and services within any society, as it can literally make the difference between life and death. It is also a very contentious issue; many liberals want to socialize healthcare, while the conservatives want to keep it at least somewhat private. In the United States, the trend of healthcare is clear: more socialization and regulation of the field. Only the most allegedly "extreme" rightists support a halt in the socialization of medicine. Any suggestion of reversing the march towards socialized medicine is immediately met with baseless accusations of "heartlessness", as if the redistribution of healthcare services is somehow compassionate. Such accusations are not worthy of a response; they are not valid criticisms of healthcare privatization and have no place in a civilized debate.

Many proponents and opponents of socialized medicine both miss the extent to which healthcare has already been socialized in the United States. Medicare, Medicaid, healthcare regulations, occupational licensing, insurance mandates, and state lines for insurance companies are all examples of coercive barriers to competition, or direct replacement of healthcare with government subsidy. It was only after the recent repeal of the Affordable Care Act (ACA), otherwise known as "Obama Care", that insurance companies have had some relief from the oppressive regulations making them nearly indistinguishable from public utilities. However, there is still thorough government involvement in healthcare that is restricting the affordability, quality, advancement, and accessibility of healthcare, which must be relinquished for ethical and practical reasons.

Objections to Private Healthcare

Many proponents of socialized medicine object to the privatization of healthcare on the grounds that it may not be accessible to everyone. According to them, healthcare is a fundamental individual right, just as life, liberty, and property, and thus the government has an imperative to subsidize healthcare for all of its citizens. The main issue with this argument is the same of all arguments involving the claim of positive rights. There *cannot* be any right to healthcare, because that "right" would conflict with the rights of others, specifically property rights and individual autonomy, both two deeply connected rights. A "right" to healthcare would imply that someone has the right to the labour and property of others, thus putting others in a slave position to the extent of a person(s) healthcare requirement(s). However, let us grant, for the sake of argument, that healthcare is a right (which it isn't). Wouldn't it then be critically important to ensure that the provider(s) of healthcare have the most incentive to be efficient and productive in the allocation of their services? Wouldn't it be better to have competition, rather than monopolization? Wouldn't it be better to ensure the maximum incentive for innovation in healthcare, making more life-saving services and technologies come to fruition than what would otherwise be available?

All of these advantages are exclusive to a privatized healthcare system, yet are rejected by the advocates of socialized medicine in favour of universality. In a free market healthcare system, not everyone would be able to afford healthcare services, just as there are those who are unable to afford other critically important goods/services. The solution, however, to this unfortunate, small minority is not the monopolization and subsidization of all healthcare; in a society devoid of taxation, as mentioned earlier, there would be maximum incentive for charitability. Private charities would be more than able to take care of the small minority of individuals who fall through the cracks of healthcare costs.

The Right to Try

Additionally, a fully privatized healthcare system would allow quicker access to various drugs or medical technologies not fully gone through testing. To the average consumer, such drugs or technologies would be unappealing, but to a near-terminal patient, they could mean the difference between life or death. These patients would have very little to lose, so such a process would be beneficial to them. Such a healthcare system could have different tiers of testing, and various types of labelling corresponding with it. In this way, a healthcare system could have faster access to potentially life-saving drugs without sacrificing consumer awareness.

Transparency and Accountability

The transparency and accountability of doctors, drug providers, etc. would be extremely thorough within a free market. Even within the regulated market of U.S healthcare, resources including WebMD.com, NJHospitalCompare.com, and PharmacyChecker.com have proliferated alongside digital technology (Heritage Foundation). These resources give patients increased information and awareness about possible health issues that could threaten them, as well as the quality of care within various hospitals and pharmacies, respectively. In order to boost their reputations, medical firms and providers would subject themselves to third-party oversight and review. Medical firms and providers not subjecting themselves to this oversight would become very suspicious to consumers, and would thus lose out on potential customers. The lack of occupational licensing within the market of healthcare would ensure ruthless competition, and thus a greater incentive for lower prices and higher quality. This is not merely speculation; the same phenomenon has coincided with the deregulation of airlines and trucking.

Some may argue that government-mandated occupational licensing is necessary for consumer safety within healthcare. Occupational licensing, however rigorous its testing, cannot guarantee that doctors will follow health and safety protocol. Occupational licensing bottlenecks competitors within a healthcare field, but it does not stop doctors from taking hazardous and unnecessary risks with their clientele.

If a doctor or medical provider makes a critical error resulting in the harm or injury of one of their clients, then this would be a matter for civil court. Lawsuits over harm and injury are a fierce deterrent of negligent or hazardous actions. As mentioned in *Law and Justice*, this kind of restitutive justice would also allow a victim to be recompensed for any harm that they have suffered at the hands of harmful medical practices. Lawsuits are not able to deter all hazardous medical practices, but neither does occupational licensing or regulation. Lawsuits, contrary to licensing and regulation do not restrict the affordability, quality, accessibility, and advancement of healthcare, and are thus perfectly legitimate, ethically and practically, for deterring healthcare malfeasance.

The Alternative to Universality

Finally, a completely privatized healthcare system is the one most conducive to the very ideal that many of the liberals are attempting to achieve through socialization. The goal of socialized healthcare, observable through the arguments made by the liberals, is safety. Liberals who want to socialize healthcare because of genuine reasons, want to have safety in numbers, so that no dispossessed individuals can fall through the cracks of healthcare costs. In a fully privatized healthcare system, the liberals would be able to enter into group insurance plans such as "Medi-Share", in which they would be able to pay collectively into the insurance pool, of which the insurance plan would apply to all the individuals within the group, and aid them in unforeseeable and unpreventable medical contingencies. Thus, it is actually a privatized, free market healthcare system that is most conducive to the liberals' goal. However, it is different from socialized healthcare in two ways. The first is that there are more than one providers of healthcare competing for clients, rather than it being monopolized. The second is that those taking part in "Medi-Share" or group insurance could not force other people to join it, as is possible in socialized healthcare. Unfortunately, this is

likely the real reason that the liberals oppose it.

Chapter 8: Education

Education is the process of integrating knowledge in preparation for life, particularly for youth. Education is of critical importance to acquiring skills, gaining understanding, and developing one's own ideas, values, and convictions. It is due to the critical importance of education that so many people support its socialization, as well as its regulation via mandatory curriculum. The irony of this passionate activism is that the socialization and regulation of education actually hinders the quality and advancement of education, and is harmful to the learning and development of the youth.

Free Enterprise vs. Socialized Education

As with any other field of free enterprise, private education is competitive. Schools and teachers have a vested interest in ensuring the effective learning of their students. If private schools do not teach students effectively, or are otherwise insufficient, then they will lose clients, thereby losing profits and endangering the business. Private schools will not survive in the free market if they are not effective at teaching and caring for students.

The financing of public education, in contrast, is unconditional. If parents or students are dissatisfied with the quality of service of the teachers, it often has no impact on their salaries. Frighteningly, dissatisfaction can actually be *beneficial* to the financial success of public school personnel. This is due to the fact that public schools are financed via public subsidy. If a public school is found to be failing in a given area, it is often used as justification to *increase* the subsidization of that school. It is thus that a destructive zero-sum game manifests. If public school teachers can perform just well enough to maintain employment, but never go above and beyond what is required of them, then there is more incentive for politicians to increase funding. Additionally, many public schools mandate the attendance of students, so that there is no way for students or parents to avoid the hazards commensurate with the existence of public education. In this way, the law declares, in effect, that the government has legitimate ownership over the minds of children. Thus, poor performance of public school teachers is actually *incentivized* by the government, and "the squeaky wheel gets the grease" so to speak.

Educational Curriculum

Mandatory curriculum for private education is also extremely hazardous. The existence of mandatory school curriculum promotes the crass insinuation that governments and regulators know how to educate students in a superior fashion to parents and teachers. Not only does the government seize private property in order to finance education (of which one may never be compensated if agents choose private education), but it also attempts to regulate matters of teaching of which government agents have no expertise or specialization in. Through mandating school curriculum, of any kind, the government commits acts worse than mere theft. It attempts to directly hijack the minds of schoolteachers, and thus the minds of children.

The totalitarian implications of public education are inescapable; if the state is to determine how much parents pay for education, what kind of school children will go to, and what content they will be taught, then children are mere automatons to be directed in whatever way the state wishes. If the government has the moral imperative to seize children from their parents, in order to inculcate them contents of its choosing with or without the consent of the parents, then the logical conclusion is that the government owns the minds of children.

Consequently, more and more children are growing up to be rabidly authoritarian and collectivist without any second thought; the state teaches children material in such a manner as to make them more sympathetic to its actions.

So-called "impartial" history is inescapably taught through a lens favourable to the state. Schools teach the "horrors" of the industrial revolution, but ignore its achievements or the horrors of the times preceding it. Governments are invariably incentivized to teach material in a manner biased in favour of state control, and biased against political freedom.

Through teaching false philosophical premises such as altruism, the government is able, metaphorically speaking, to get whole generations of children to eat out of its hand. It is beyond shocking to witness how eager and automatically today's college students to blindly follow their professors' political agendas. Students will protest free speech, use violent, physicalistic tactics against dissenters, and will promote political philosophies as abhorrent as communism and anarchism. But this is not because they are "rebellious"; it represents their blind allegiance to *exactly* what the older generation told them to do. It is in this manner that the state is able to indoctrinate, manipulate, and brainwash children into becoming dedicated statists who will fight passionately against freedom and individual rights.

Chapter 9: Transportation Networks

Nearly all ideologies on the political compass begin their discussion of transportation with the implicit assumption that the state is the institution best equipped to build, maintain, and manage transportation infrastructure such as roads, bridges, railways, etc. The general political debate then usually centres on *what* types of infrastructure the state ought to build. In reality, this assumption could not be further from the truth, as free enterprise is the system best equipped to building, maintaining, and managing all types of transportation infrastructure. In fact, private companies already own some types of transportation infrastructure traditionally delegated to the state, such as highways and railways. However, there are still certain types believed to be exclusively made possible by the doings of the government, and which would allegedly disappear in a free enterprise system. It is believed that, while the free market can manage *some* goods correctly, the construction of narrow, painted strips of asphalt, for instance, is out of its capability.

State vs. Free Enterprise Transportation Networks

Transportation infrastructure, like all costs of living under free enterprise, would be subject to private ownership. Grand or humble, these networks would be built, maintained, and managed by private companies, and would thus be open to competition, avoiding the many risks and difficulties associated with state management including moral hazard, universal access, and misallocation of resources due to the effects of the economic calculation problem.

Government administered transportation infrastructure tends to be morally hazardous in its phenomenon of universal access. In essence, universal access to a particular good reduces the incentive to maintain or respect its existence. Public access to infrastructure does not disincentivize users from littering, vandalizing, etc. the particular good in question, due to the fact that they have virtually no stake in the good itself. The moral hazard of universal ownership tends to leave roads in ugly, abused condition and disrepair.

Objections to Private Transportation Networks

Some may object to the privatization of roads, bridges, railways, etc. on the grounds that they would be taken care of poorly: i.e. abandoned, ignored, etc. However, there would actually be an *increased* incentive to maintain such infrastructure properly in a free enterprise system, since the businesses owning that infrastructure would be subject to competition. For example, if BlueCorp owns a highway connecting Tokyo and Yokohama, and takes care of it poorly, causing it to be in disrepair, the number of people willing to utilize that particular highway would dramatically decrease, decimating profits for BlueCorp. If the competitor of BlueCorp, RedCorp owns a different highway connecting the two cities, and RedCorp puts in painstaking effort to keep it in pristine quality and condition, RedCorp would effectively co-opt all of the customers of BlueCorp all else being equal. If, however, the Japanese government owned and managed both highways, and left them in complete disrepair, then everyday Japanese citizens would be left completely without any form of recourse. They could attempt to petition the government to repair the highways, but if the Japanese government does not repair the roads, nothing else could be done. The Japanese government, at this point, wields a true monopoly over highways. If private businesses attempt to build highways to compete, the government could simply seize the property (assuming the Japanese government is legally permitted to do so).

Some object to private roads on the grounds that they would be likely to monopolize spontaneously. This however is just as dubious as monopolization in any other field of industry. If BlueCorp tried to buy up its competitors, RedCorp and GreenCorp in an attempt to establish ownership over all roads, its competitors RedCorp and GreenCorp would realize their opportunity to a) charge exorbitant prices for their infrastructure, or b) refuse to sell their roads and undercut the bloated giant. The latter would be the more effective medium to long-term strategy for RedCorp and GreenCorp, and would thus be incentivized to prudent competitors. Even in the nightmare scenario in which BlueCorp owned all roads connecting Tokyo and Yokohama, RedCorp and GreenCorp could still construct new roads beside, or alternatively dig tunnels under, or build bridges over BlueCorp's roads.

Additionally, BlueCorp would not just be competing with other road companies; within free enterprise, it is true that roads would compete with each other, but they also compete with trains, planes, helicopters, tunnels, paths, and sometimes even boats in order to satisfy the transportation needs of consumers. This would ensure ruthless competition within transportation industries even assuming little competition between road companies themselves.

Financing of Transportation Networks

Another objection to private roads is that the logistics of financing such ventures (tolls, premiums, etc.) would be nearly impossible. According to the critics of private roads, every driver would need to pay a toll for approximately every fifty feet of road they drove across. Based on this argument, one would presume that private roads would waste time and money. While this argument could be given the benefit of the doubt in primitive, pre-industrial societies, to make this argument in the digital age is spurious and ridiculous. Many contemporary applications for digital goods such as *Google Maps* and GPS (Global Positioning System) already use satellite technology to determine a car's position in relation to landmarks, streets, etc. Companies could easily develop applications utilizing this technology to calculate the total amount of money to be paid with ease and impeccable precision. Additionally, companies could utilize digital trackers to keep record of the number of cars, specific clients, and distance travelled, and then determine how much money is due to be paid. This money could then be paid digitally, avoiding all inconveniences of tolls. However, even without this technology, this difficulty could easily be avoided through a road company premium system. For example, RedCorp could charge premiums for registered clients, allowing them to travel that company's roads with ease. If clients frequently use the roads of RedCorp and GreenCorp, they could alternatively sell multi-company premiums. Finally, road owning enterprises could also negotiate with nearby businesses, so that the nearby businesses pay for the upkeep of the road in exchange for the road's appeal to consumers by allowing fast and safe transport. This would allow consumers a great deal of convenience in exchange for only a slight increase in the cost of consumer products. The problem of infrastructure financing could be addressed effectively with even the most rudimentary level of thought and innovation.

Advantages to Privatized Transportation Networks

In addition to having greater incentive for higher quality, private roads would also be immune from the issues associated with central planning in regard to the economic calculation problem. Since governments do not rely on profits from their infrastructure, they do not have to worry about *where* they build the roads. This is hazardous in that it can easily lead to the misallocation of valuable resources, money, labour, etc. required to build the roads. Privatized networks of roads could easily avoid this problem in the exact same way as mentioned earlier in *The Economy*, in regards to the economic calculation problem. In essence, a business will keep constructing roads as long as it is profitable to do so. In this way, businesses responsible for the construction of roads would be able to allocate resources appropriately, building more or fewer of them depending on how many potential customers they have. These businesses could gain this data through surveying various towns, cities, etc. Road-building enterprises would build many roads in highly populated areas, where the demand for roads is high. However, they would not build roads in areas where almost no one lives; i.e. ghost towns, wasteland, etc. This would reduce total road traffic in urban areas, as there would be many more options and routes to take than when left to government planning, and would thus make travel easier and more convenient. It is in this way that the free market can avoid the misallocation of resources in infrastructure due to central planning. Private roads would also save money for the average consumer. Instead of having to pay taxes to subsidize all roads, consumers could choose *which* roads to sponsor according to their own individual transportation needs.

There are hardly any political issues so deceptively simple as transportation infrastructure, and none so unfairly maligned, disparaged and misrepresented. Opponents of free enterprise ask, "Who would build the roads?" This question brings with it the crass insinuation that the proponents of free enterprise are so intellectually lazy that they have not once taken the most rudimentary thought in analysing and evaluating the issue of transportation infrastructure in a free market. Opponents of free enterprise ask this question as if there is no answer or reasonable explanation for such transportation infrastructure in a free enterprise society. In reality, this question is comparable to a volleyball game, in which a softball is lobbed straight down the middle of the field. If one is able to get past the superficial attacks (not even criticisms) made against the concept of private transportation infrastructure, one can see that the free market is not only more moral, but more practical in fulfilling this task than the state.

Chapter 10: The Environment

Nearly all political perspectives, whether implicitly or explicitly, believe that free enterprise is the nemesis of the natural world. Free enterprise is blamed almost exclusively for environmental damage, disasters, etc. Opponents of free enterprise evade the fact that environmental destruction is possible within any other social system: anarchism, communism, fascism, or anything in between. In fact, there are many ways in which the legal implementation of private property is actually *beneficial* to preserving the wildlife, territories, etc. of nature.

The Tragedy of The Commons

Firstly, free enterprise avoids the phenomenon of the tragedy of the commons: as goods are owned exclusively, it incentivizes rational, long-term planning and decreases time preference. However, if goods are owned universally; i.e. un-owned, there becomes increased incentive for overconsumption and an increase in time preference. This basic law of economics applies to all goods, including wildlife itself. If a forest, for example, is universally owned, then there becomes an incentive to plunder and loot it as quickly as possible, for all parties involved. Thus, universal ownership is completely unsustainable for the preservation of the environment; there is no incentive to care for or maintain it, especially when one's efforts will be sabotaged by the actions of others. If that same forest is privately owned, no such sabotage is permitted. Thus, there becomes an increased incentive to put it to good use. There may be some artificial intervention on such property, but the owner(s) of that property would have the time and security to carefully plan out their construction so as to not excessively intrude on it. In many instances, such property would become private parks, in which visitors could pay to visit and enjoy such unspoiled estates.

Pollution

Pollution is an aspect of the environment to which many regard free enterprise as being unable to manage. According to many environmentalists, government-imposed regulations on private businesses are necessary to curb the toxic destruction caused by pollution. In reality, civil court systems can fulfil the same role as government-imposed regulations, but without the use of prior restraint, and thus without the violation of physical property rights. For reference, prior restraint is the process of preventing someone from taking a certain action as an out-of-context absolute. Prior restraint does not take into account the specific facts of each case, and thus does not account for any harm (or lack thereof) done to others.

Environmental Regulations vs. Civil Justice

Imagine what the United States would look like tomorrow if the government outlawed *all* pollution in the country, including carbon emissions. The result would be complete economic depression and impoverishment. Imagine this on a smaller scale, and you have environmental regulations. This is not to say that there should be no intervention if businesses start dumping toxic waste on other people's property. That is not the justice of free enterprise, but the chaos of anarchy. The government *can* legitimately punish businesses for such acts, but it must do so through the proper legal process, and for the sake of actual victims of malfeasance, rather than the whims of bureaucrats. A practical example will help illustrate this issue clearly:

Johnny has a business selling fish from his riverside home downstream from a BlueCorp factory. The BlueCorp factory, in its process of production, puts chemicals into the river, which eventually make their way to the part of the river on Johnny's property. The chemicals from the BlueCorp factory poison the fish on Johnny's property, causing his property to be damaged and his fishing business to be ruined. Johnny, because of the harm he suffered, takes legal action against BlueCorp, filing a tort lawsuit, which wins him a sum of money, equivalent to the damage he suffered. As mentioned earlier in *Law and Justice*, restitutive justice simultaneously punishes a criminal offender for their harmful actions, and compensates the victim for the harm suffered. After the lawsuit, Johnny is able to start his own business selling firewood, and BlueCorp is more averse to allowing negligence in their production process, fearing another lawsuit.

This is the legitimate role of the government in a free enterprise society; not to act as a paternal parent, but instead as a policeman who can adjudicate various criminal cases when and where they occur. It is in this way that businesses would be deterred from taking actions harmful to others, but not punished for taking actions harmful to no one. A system of private property makes such criminal cases extremely easy and simple to adjudicate; it is clear who owns what and is responsible for what in every instance.

Universal vs. Private Ownership of Nature

Under universal ownership, however, this type of precise adjudication system is not possible. On one hand, BlueCorp would have a right to do whatever it wants with the environment. On the other hand, Johnny would have the right not to have the river damaged by BlueCorp. A civil court system, in a vacuum of ownership, could not resolve disputes of that kind. This, among other reasons, is why private ownership is necessary for achieving a just society.

This is why public parks and wildlife preserves tend to be so badly abused. Litter, irresponsibility, and negligence plague them. But this is not inevitable; under private ownership, parties who do not comply with basic care of the property can be physically removed via security, police, or even military forces in severe contingencies. This would lead to a much greater deterrence of irresponsible and negligent behaviour on the part of visitors, tourists, etc. On the part of owners, the economic incentive for environmental preservation would be to gain a return of one's ownership of the property. Destructive and negligent actions on the part of property owners would result in a net decrease of value in the properties' worth all else being equal. If this happens, the owners cannot reap the capital value of the properties and thus lose massive economic value via opportunity cost. Private property creates an economic and legal incentive to preserve and care for the environment.

Climate Change

As humans continue to utilize fossil fuels to power transportation, machinery, and production, an unintended environmental externality manifests: climate change. While regarded as the originator of this environmental hazard, free enterprise only has a coincidental relationship to it. Under any other social system: anarchism, communism, fascism, or anything in between, humans continue to utilize fossil fuels the same way they do today. It is only the free enterprise system that is capable of allowing humans to escape their reliance on carbon-emitting technologies, unlike the social systems which hamper and restrict technological innovation.

Green technologies, like any other type of innovation are dependant on capital investment, unconventional thinking and planning, and an incentive for profit to ever come into fruition. The only way a government can "help" the origination green technologies is to fulfil its proper role within society: protecting individual rights. Through protecting intellectual and physical property rights, a government can make the origination of new green tech viable and desirable for companies to partake in. As the creator of green technology has the exclusive right to the product of his/her mind, he/she has the most incentive to dedicate time, resources, and effort into the origination of these ventures.

It is also critically important that the government relinquish any infringements it places upon property rights including regulations and taxes. It is through the abolition of these infringements that companies will have an increased incentive to develop green technologies, as they will be able to innovate in and profit from these technologies to the greatest possible extent.

Free enterprise would also help to reduce carbon emissions even as agents currently utilize this technology. As mentioned earlier in *Infrastructure*, privatized transportation networks are able to avoid the moral hazard created by public transportation networks such as roads. But this would also help the environment by reducing nationwide carbon emissions in two ways. Since private roads avoid the moral hazard of state managed transportation networks, in which citizens are charged whether or not they use the roads or how much they use them, private roads would incentivize drivers to take shorter, more efficient routes to their desired destination. Private roads would also incentivize individuals travelling to a common location to carpool, which would result in a net decrease in carbon emissions all else being equal. It is in these ways that private roads would be beneficial to the environment, as opposed to the moral hazard of state administered transportation systems. Because of these reasons, in addition to many others, environmentalists should be clamouring for the privatization of roads, if they do truly value the environment.

Conclusion

The historical, present-day, and future success of free enterprise is simply a derivative of its proper, logical, and incontestable political principles. As demonstrated in *The Objectivist Manifesto*, free enterprise is the most free, just system in human history.

It is the freedom and protection of individual rights of free enterprise that has allowed agents within it to be extremely productive, innovative, and beneficial not only to themselves, but to others in the process. The least successful and prosperous within free enterprise gain enormously from the success and productiveness of the most successful and prosperous. New inventions and companies created by leading entrepreneurs and businessmen provides opportunity and benefit to the impoverished via employment, technologies, knowledge, etc.

Free enterprise is the social system most conducive to the prosperity of even the poorest, but that is not its primary justification. Its primary justification is that it bans the initiation of physical force within human relationships, which is the practical implementation of individual rights. Free enterprise is based on the principle that no agent(s) may seize an unearned value from any another agent(s). Agent(s) may gain unearned value(s) as a secondary consequence of another agent(s)'s success, but cannot gain it at the expense of the originator.

Free enterprise *does* create inequality; as agents are free from coercion at the hands of both criminals and the state, they will make dramatically different life choices from one another and will thus have wildly different results. In free enterprise, market forces serve to incentivize the most rational, productive behaviour. Merit, not political pull, determines success, and agents will get just as far as their work ethic will take them. Free enterprise is a social system where every agent gets what he/she deserves, either positive or negative, and cannot negate the consequences of one's actions. If any political activist, group, or ideology condemns free enterprise for creating inequality, this is why: free enterprise is the only social system compatible with the principle of justice.

Once the truth and moral superiority of free enterprise has been established, the only question that remains is how best to go about implementing and devising it. It is only after the objections to the ends of free enterprise have been refuted, that the means of achieving it can be rigorously debated.

The political establishment of every society in every place and in every era can be traced back to its most fundamental philosophical premises.

To the extent that a society embraces altruism, the principle of self-sacrifice, it will move further to political collectivism. If it is moral and necessary to sacrifice one's own interests to the demands and needs of others, then surely moral agents should be *forced* to do so. Freedom and individual rights cannot be justified on the basis of altruism; the moral theory does not permit such concepts. And if a society embraces altruism fully and completely, then totalitarian domination will reign, as was embodied in Nazi Germany, Soviet Russia, and Mao's China throughout the 20th century, and is embodied in communist Cuba or Hugo Chavez's Venezuela in the 21st century.

Likewise, the extent to which a society embraces egoism, or moral selfishness is the extent to which it will embrace individual rights and capitalism. If the moral good constitutes acting to one's own self-interest, which can only be done through independent, rational thought, then it follows that moral agents must be free from coercion in order to pursue the moral good; moral agents need to be free from coercion to utilize reason. This principle was most closely embodied, implicitly, in the foundation of the United States of America, which was the freest, wealthiest, and most moral society in human history. But the political exponent of egoism was formulated and embodied explicitly in America; the stated purpose of the United States government was to protect individual rights.

There was always a discrepancy between the ethical and political aspects of America's philosophy; Americans believed in freedom, but couldn't formulate or explain why. Thus, many Americans ended up turning to religion, faith, and superstition to retroactively justify political freedom. The slogan "god given rights" took over in philosophical discourse, as Americans became more and more disconnected from the true philosophical basis of their society.

Religion and freedom is an explosive, radioactive mixture, which results in evasions, distortions, and incomprehensible panic. The two principles cannot exist fully and consistently within the same being, nor within the same society. Religion commands mindless and faithful obedience to the omniscient dictates of god. But what is one to do if or when these dictates conflict with individual rights? Religion prescribes the discarding of reason, regarding it as infinitely dwarfed by the endless intellect of the supreme creator. Without reason, there is no justification for selfishness. Without selfishness, there is no justification for freedom.

Thus, a culture's philosophical premises reach deeper than even a shared theory of morality (ethics). The moral theory of a culture itself is based upon a theory of knowledge, known as epistemology. The implicit epistemological theory of *The Objectivist Manifesto* is composed of reason and sense perception. It is only if agents can grasp the percepts (letters) within this book, and formulate such sensory data into synthesized information that they can gain any knowledge from it. Otherwise, no books can be of any use to anyone.

Modern western culture, however, will tell you that this theory of knowledge is incorrect. Many professors and teachers claim that the senses lie to and deceive human beings, and that reason is simply an arbitrary construct or game with no relationship to reality. Many individuals accept the premises that emotions are an efficacious means of gaining knowledge, and that some amount of religious faith is necessary for moral integrity.

In most types of debates or arguments, it is possible to point to a more basic principle or fact, which possesses proper application to the issue at hand. But epistemology is a type of science, which has no deeper reference point (epistemology is tied to metaphysics, but it is necessary to utilize reason in order to know reality). Thus, the advocates of "alternative" theories of knowledge actually put themselves outside the bounds of coherent argumentation. By rejecting reason, such agents disable themselves from being able to coherently discuss any theories of knowledge. *The Objectivist Manifesto* starts with its ethical, rather than epistemological analysis because it is impossible to convince someone that reason is efficacious. All that this book can do is point in the right direction, and say "look".

But if one accepts reason as the only efficacious means of gaining knowledge, and makes no errors in its application in ethics and politics, one must conclude that the only social system proper to rational beings is free enterprise, in which agents can act freely in pursuit of their own rational self-interest without the interference of physical force. Thus, the only possibility of achieving free enterprise purposefully and consistently is a philosophical revolution. Specifically, it must be a metaphysical and epistemological revolution; reason cannot be based in a vacuum; it is derived from the nature of reality, which is itself objective, whole, and non-contradictory.

Such a philosophical revolution must begin in within any institutions or networks of accumulating and sharing knowledge. Academic institutions such as schools, colleges, and universities are an important place to start; they are critically influential on the developing years of youth, and will shape generations to come, for better or for worse. Universities must discard their Kantian, postmodern epistemological theories in favour of a rational, Aristotelian approach.

The Internet can also be utilized to help share the philosophical ideas necessary to achieve liberty. Internet communication is advantageous in that it is not limited by location; anyone can communicate with anyone in seconds thanks to this technology. Unfortunately, the Internet has not been put to good use in a significant degree. Most philosophical actors on the Internet continuously spread and proliferate irrational and erroneous ideas, which is responsible more than ever for our cultural degradation. The Internet serves as a tool to amplify the influence of whatever philosophical voices currently exist. In today's irrational and depraved culture, the Internet has been weaponized as a means of furthering, not preventing, the west's philosophical collapse. But this is not inevitable; a culture with the right philosophy and ideological confidence could not only strengthen and bolster itself, but also spread its own influence to the rest of the world.

Any philosophical renaissance, whatever its means, must be achieved in a bottom-up fashion. It must begin in education and academia before its political implications can manifest. Politics is the derivative of philosophy; this process cannot be achieved in reverse. The privatization of education would certainly *quicken* such a renaissance, but it could not act as its fundamental catalyst. The right ideas must be accepted for the privatization of education to even *occur* in the first place, unless by accident. But once such ideas are widely accepted, with their full, consistent implication, the political change would flow automatically. An increasing number of voters and politicians would embrace Ayn Rand's philosophy, and would thus be increasingly motivated to implement changes and policies conducive to liberty, including deregulation, tax abolition, and the relinquishment of government subsidization, until a proper, rights-respecting government has been established.

Such a philosophical renaissance would not be impending from the perspective of my lifetime; it would occur slowly and gradually, in the range of centuries. However, some important gains can still be made in the short term, and any progress towards freedom, however small, is still beneficial to any and every rational being, who by its nature requires it in order to achieve any and all ethical values.

However, this is not the fundamental purpose of this book. Such a fundamental cultural change would be miraculous; in all likelihood, the west is due for a long, slow decline. Immanuel Kant's philosophical ideas are so thoroughly ingrained in western academia that attempting to change it directly would be deadening and futile. Instead, this book should be taken as an examination of the world as it *could* be and *should* be. This is not to say that it is utopian; even in a rational society there would still be crime, and there would still be depravity. But as is demonstrated in the last five chapters of this book, free enterprise has the least incentive for both of these, and the most incentive for rational, egoistic behaviour.

The real purpose behind *The Objectivist Manifesto* is to serve my own selfish interests. This book contains within it the ideas that could change the world for the better, but this is merely a secondary benefit. Writing and editing this book has brought me personal happiness; it has allowed my ideas and thoughts to manifest themselves in a coherent, organized form, allowing me to show, with unparalleled clarity, the justification and benefits of a free, individualistic society. I find meaning and purpose from creating articulate and persuasive works such as this one, and I will continue to build upon and expand them for my many decades to come. Hopefully, gentle reader, you have found similar meaning in poring over the many pages in this book, and will be inspired from it to create value, pursue happiness, and live selfishly.

Resources

Introduction:

Williamson, Kevin. "Socialism and Nationalism: Allies, Not Rivals". *The Politically Incorrect Guide to Socialism*. Washington DC. United States. Regnery Publishing Inc. 2011. Page 180.

"President Franklin D. Roosevelt and the New Deal". *Wikiquote*. Online. https://en.wikiquote.org/wiki/Wikiquote:Transwiki/American_history_quotes_New_Deal

Kiely, Eugene. "'You Didn't Build That,' Uncut and Unedited". *Fact Check*. July 23, 2012. Online. https://www.factcheck.org/2012/07/you-didnt-build-that-uncut-and-unedited/

Chapter 1: Ethics

Rand, Ayn. "The Virtue of Selfishness | A New Concept of Egoism". United States. New American Library. 1964.

Chapter 2: Property

Rand, Ayn. "Capitalism: The Unknown Ideal". United States. New American Library. 1966.

Chapter 3: Government

Gross, Samuel R., O'Brien, Barbara, Hu, Chen, Kennedy, Edward H.

"Rate of false conviction of criminal defendants who are sentenced to death".

Proceedings of the National Academy of Sciences of the United States of

America. May 20, 2014. Online.

http://www.pnas.org/content/111/20/7230

Binswanger, Harry. "Anarchism vs. Objectivism". *The Harry*

Binswanger List. Online. July 20, 2011.

http://www.hblist.com/anarchy.htm

Chapter 4: Constitution

"Constitution of the United States". *United States Senate.* Online.

https://www.senate.gov/civics/constitution_item/constitution.htm#amdt_2_(1

791)

"2017 Estimates Show Vehicle Fatalities Topped 40,000 for Second

Straight Year". *National Safety Council.* Online.

https://www.nsc.org/road-safety/safety-topics/fatality-estimates

"Number of murder victims in the United States in 2017, by weapon".

Statista. Online.

https://www.statista.com/statistics/195325/murder-victims-in-the-us-by-

weapon-used/

"H.R.3162 - Uniting and Strengthening America by Providing Appropriate Tools Required to Intercept and Obstruct Terrorism (USA PATRIOT ACT) Act of 2001". *Congress*. Online. https://www.congress.gov/bill/107th-congress/house-bill/3162

"NSA Spying". *Electronic Frontier Foundation*. Online. https://www.eff.org/nsa-spying

Bynum, Justin. "What are antitrust laws". *Investopedia*. Online. Feb 12, 2018. https://www.investopedia.com/ask/answers/09/antitrust-law.asp

The Editors of Encyclopedia Britannica. "Sherman Antitrust Act". *Encyclopedia Britannica*. Online. https://www.britannica.com/event/Sherman-Antitrust-Act

Chapter 5: Warfare

Pattison, James. "Using volunteer forces, rather than conscripts or private contractors, is the most legitimate method for organizing a military". *The London School of Economics and Political Science*. Online. May 8, 2013. http://blogs.lse.ac.uk/europpblog/2013/05/08/using-all-volunteer-forces-most-legitimate-military-private-contractors-conscription-morality-james-pattison/

Chapter 6: The Economy

Salter, Alex. "Economics and the Calculation Problem". *Foundation for Economic Education*. Oct 29, 2012. Online.

https://fee.org/articles/economics-and-the-calculation-problem/

"Child Labor" *History*. Oct 27, 2009. Online

https://www.history.com/topics/industrial-revolution/child-labor

Chapter 7: Healthcare

Wilson, Dr. Lawrence. "The Case Against Medical And All Other Occupational Licensing". *Dr L Wilson*. Online.

https://www.drlwilson.com/Articles/licensing.htm

Capretta, James. Dayaratna, Kevin."Compelling Evidence Makes The Case For a Market-Driven Health Care System". *Heritage Foundation*. Dec 20, 2013. Online.

https://www.heritage.org/health-care-reform/report/compelling-evidence-makes-the-case-market-driven-health-care-system